200 healthy curries

hamlyn | all color cookbook

200 healthy curries

Sunil Vijayakar

An Hachette UK Company
www.hachette.co.uk

First published in Great Britain in 2012 by Hamlyn,
a division of Octopus Publishing Group Ltd.
Endeavour House, 189 Shaftesbury Avenue
London WC2H 8JY
www.octopusbooks.co.uk
www.octopusbooksusa.com

Distributed in the US by Hachette Book Group USA
237 Park Avenue, New York NY 10017 USA

Distributed in Canada by Canadian Manda Group
165 Dufferin Street, Toronto, Ontario, Canada M6K 3H6

ISBN: 978-0-600-62699-2

Printed and bound in China

10 9 8 7 6 5 4 3 2 1

People with known nut allergies should avoid recipes
containing nuts or nut derivatives, and vulnerable people
should avoid dishes containing raw or lightly cooked eggs.

Standard level spoon and cup measurements
are used in all recipes.

Ovens should be preheated to the specified temperature—
if using a convection oven, follow the manufacturer's
instructions for adjusting the time and temperature.
Broilers should also be preheated.

Fresh herbs should be used unless otherwise stated.

Large eggs should be used unless otherwise stated.

Some of the recipes in this book have previously appeared
in other titles published by Hamlyn.

contents

introduction

introduction

Originating from the South Indian Tamil word *kari*, which means gravy or sauce, the word "curry" literally refers to the spice blend used to flavor a dish. The word is now evolving to describe a wide variety of saucy, spiced dishes from all over India, Southeast Asia, and even as far as Japan. We once used the word to describe an entire cuisine, but recently we have begun to discover the true diversity of this flavorsome food, and we are being introduced to authentic recipes from the many countries that provide spicy dishes that fall under the "curry" umbrella.

A common perception is that a curry is a hot and spicy dish. Yes, you can eat a curry that will blow your socks off but, on the whole, most curry recipes are delicate and highly sophisticated, containing a balanced blend of spices and herbs.

As food lovers today, we have embraced curries from all over the world and count them among our favorite foods. There is nothing more satisfying to me than producing a rich, aromatic curry to share with friends and family. All you need are a pantry of spices and ingredients, some simple equipment, and to learn some basic techniques.

healthy favorites

Unfortunately, many curries contain a lot of oil, butter, and cream, which are blended with herbs and spices to create rich but unhealthy dishes. However, the delicious recipes in this book will show you that you can cook healthy curries without compromising on flavor and taste. We have re-created favorite curries—and some more unusual ones—without relying on unhealthy ingredients. We use them in much smaller quantities than usual and replace them with healthier options, such as peanut oil, which is much lower in saturated fat than ghee, sunflower oil, or butter. We have used fat-free plain yogurt and reduced-fat coconut milk instead of cream and butter.

We have also omitted or reduced sugar and replaced it with agave syrup. Sweeter than honey, this organic, fat-free sweetener can replace sugar in many recipes—you only need a small amount. Likewise, when seasoning your dishes, be sure to use salt sparingly because a high intake can contribute to high blood pressure and heart disease.

basic ingredients

You can buy most of the ingredients you need for the recipes in this book in any large grocery store. Markets and ethnic food stores are great places to find the more unusual items, and they will stock large packages of spices at good prices. You can also order "exotic" ingredients from speciality Web sites and have them delivered to your door.

dry spices

The flavor of dry spices decreases with time, so buy them in small quantities and use them quickly for the best results.

amchoor

Dried mango powder, used as a souring agent in Indian curries. Substitute with a little lemon juice or tamarind paste if unavailable.

asafetida

Also known as devil's dung, this plant resin can be bought in a lump or dried and ground in powder form. It is strong in flavor and used in tiny amounts in lentil dishes. You can use garlic or onion powder as a substitute.

cardamom

This is usually used whole, in its pod, as an aromatic to flavor rice and curries. You can also use the little black seeds inside the pods on their own, by crushing them and using as part of a spice mixture or for a garam masala.

cassia

Also known as Chinese cinnamon, cassia is an aromatic tree bark, which can be bought as sticks, rolled bark, or powder form. It has a coarser texture and stronger flavor than cinnamon does.

chile

Whole dried red chiles add the fiery heat to a curry. Dried red pepper flakes tend to have a milder flavor and chili powders made from ground dried chiles vary in heat, ranging from mild or medium to hot.

cinnamon

This sweet and warming aromatic spice comes from the bark of a tree and is available as sticks or rolled bark. Also widely used in ground powder form.

cloves

These aromatic dried buds from an evergreen tree can be used whole or ground to a powder.

coriander

The small, pale brown seeds of the coriander plant have a fresh, citrus flavor. Available whole or ground, they form the base of many curry pastes and dry spice mixes.

cumin

Essential in Asian cooking, these small elongated brown seeds are used whole or ground, and have a distinctive, warm, pungent aroma. Whole seeds may be dry-roasted and sprinkled over a dish just before serving.

curry powders

Store-bought curry powders are available and there are many different varieties, depending on the spice mix. Some are simply labeled mild, medium, or hot, but there are many specific mixes, such as tandoori spice mix or Madras curry powder.

fennel seeds

These small, pale green seeds have a subtle licorice flavor and are used as a flavoring in some spice mixes.

fenugreek seeds

Usually square in shape, these tiny, shiny yellow seeds are used widely in pickles and ground into spice mixes for curries.

garam masala

This common spice mix is usually added to a dish at the end of cooking time. A classic garam masala mix comprises cardamom, cloves, cumin, peppercorns, cinnamon, and nutmeg. See page 78 for recipe.

mustard seeds

Black, brown, or yellow, these tiny round seeds are used as a flavoring and are often fried in oil until they "pop" to impart a mellow, nutty flavor.

nigella seeds

Also known as black onion seeds or *kalonji*, these tiny, mat black, oval seeds are most frequently used to flavor breads and pickles.

saffron

These deep orange strands are the dried stamens from a particular type of crocus and are used to give rice dishes and desserts a musky fragrance and golden color.

star anise

These dark brown, flower-shape seed pods have a licorice-like flavor. Anise seed or Chinese five-spice powder are substitutes.

turmeric

This bright yellow-orange rhizome is widely available as a dried, ground powder. Turmeric has a warm, musky flavor and is used in small quantities to add flavor and colour to lentil and rice dishes and curries.

fresh herbs & aromatics

It is essential to have a good selection of fresh herbs and aromatics on hand when making various different curries. Always buy the freshest ingredients you can find. Ethnic food stores are good places to buy aromatics, such as Thai basil, lemon grass, kaffir lime leaves, cilantro, mint, and curry leaves, because they usually have a wide selection of fresh produce available at good prices. In case you have any leftovers, chiles, lemon grass, curry leaves, and kaffir lime leaves all freeze well for future use.

chiles

Fresh green and red chiles are used in many types of curries to give heat and flavor. Much of the heat resides in the pith and seeds, so if you want to enjoy the chile taste with less heat, make a long slit down the length of the chile and carefully scrape out and discard the pith and seeds before slicing or chopping the flesh.

garlic
One of the essential flavors used in cooking all over the world, garlic cooked with ginger and onion forms the base of many curries. It is used sliced, crushed, or grated.

ginger
Another indispensable aromatic, fresh ginger root has a fresh, peppery flavor and is used in both savory and sweet dishes.

kaffir lime leaves
The leaves from the knobbly kaffir lime are highly aromatic. When used in a curry, they are usually finely shredded, but they are sometimes left whole. They freeze well and can be used straight from the freezer.

lemon grass
Known as *sere* in Indonesia, *serai* in Malaysia, *takrai* in Thailand, and *tanglad* in the Phillipines, this green grass is used for its citrus flavor and aroma. It can be used whole by bruising the bottom of the stalk, or it can be finely sliced or chopped. Remove the tough outer leaves before slicing or chopping because they can be fibrous.

cilantro
The parsley of the East, fresh cilantro is used widely in Asian cooking. Often the delicate leaves are used to flavor dishes, but the stems and roots can also be used, especially in Thai curry pastes.

curry leaves
These highly aromatic leaves are used fresh in Indian and Southeast Asian cooking. They come attached to stems in sprays and are pulled off the stems before use. Fresh curry leaves freeze well and can be used straight from the freezer.

galangal
This rhizome is used in the same way as its cousin ginger in savory dishes. It is peeled and cut into fine slivers or finely chopped. You can use fresh ginger root instead if you can't find any galangal.

onions
This humble vegetable forms the base of many curries. Sliced or chopped, it is usually slowly fried before the other ingredients are added. Store onions in a wire basket in the kitchen at room temperature.

shallots

These small, sweet, and pungent members of the onion family are widely used in Southeast Asian cooking. To peel them, slice them in half and only then remove the outer skin.

Thai basil

Found in Asian food stores, this delicate herb is used to garnish and flavor curries. You can substitute regular basil if you cannot find any.

other useful ingredients

coconut milk and coconut cream

Widely used in Asian cooking, canned coconut milk is readily available. It is added to curries to impart a rich, creamy texture. Coconut cream, used in other countries, is a thicker, richer version. Substitute with coconut milk, not the sweetened cream sold for alcoholic drinks.

chickpea flour

Also known as *besan*, this pale yellow flour, made from dried chickpeas, is used widely for thickening and binding, as well as being the main ingredient in savory batters.

palm sugar

Known as *jaggery* in India and *nam tan peep* in Thailand, this is the sugar produced from the sap of various kinds of palms. Sold in cakes or cans, palm sugar has a deep, caramel flavor and is light brown in color. It is used in curries to balance the spices. You can use any brown sugar as a substitute.

shrimp paste

This pungent preserve used in Asian cooking is made by pounding shrimp with salt and letting it decompose. It has a powerful aroma, which disappears when cooked. Anchovy paste can be used as a substitute.

sweet chili sauce

This sweet and mild sauce is made from red chiles, sugar, garlic, and vinegar.

tamarind paste

Used as a souring agent in curries, the paste from the tamarind pod can be used straight from the jar. You can also buy it in semi-dried pulp form, which needs to be soaked in warm water and strained before use.

Thai fish sauce

Also known as *nam pla*, this sauce is made from the liquid extracted from salted, fermented fish and is one of the main ingredients in Thai cooking.

cooking perfect rice

Rice is the basic accompaniment to curries served all over the world and makes a perfect foil to the spices. There are many different techniques for cooking rice. One of the simplest is the absorption method, where the rice is cooked in in a covered saucepan with a measured amount of liquid until all the liquid has been absorbed. As the liquid is absorbed, steam finishes the cooking, and the rice is tender and fluffy. For alternative ways of cooking rice, see pages 104 and 156.

Cooking perfect rice is easy if you follow these steps. For the best results, measure the rice and water accurately in a measuring cup.

step one

Rinse the rice in a few changes of cold running water. The rinsing removes any loose starch and will make the rice less sticky.

Usually, you can get good results without soaking your rice. If using older rice, however, soak it in cold water for 15–30 minutes, because this makes the grains less brittle and prone to breakage. Soaking is also traditional for basmati rice, because it helps the rice expand to its maximum length during cooking.

Whether you soak it or not, be sure to drain your rice thoroughly after rinsing or you'll be using more water during cooking than you intended.

step two

As stated above, the absorption method is the simplest way to cook rice. The key to this method is figuring out the correct amount of water or stock. The general rule is to use 1½ to 1¾ cups of water (or stock) to each cup of basmati or long-grain white rice, but you may need to experiment a little to find the amount you like best. Brown rice requires more water, while short-grain rice requires less. Keep in mind that more water gives you softer, stickier rice and less water results in firmer rice.

A heat diffuser is an important piece of equipment to use when cooking rice, because it will distribute the heat evenly under the saucepan and prevent it from burning. The other important element is a heavy saucepan to prevent scorching on the bottom, with a tight-fitting lid to keep the steam in. If your lid fits loosely, put a piece of aluminum foil or a clean dish cloth between the lid and the pan.

step three

Put the rice in the saucepan with the measured amount of liquid and bring it to a boil. Cover tightly and reduce the heat to low. After 12–15 minutes, the liquid should have been absorbed, and the rice just tender.

If you served the rice now, you'd find the top layer dry and fluffy, and the bottom moist and fragile. Here's where you need patience: Remove the pan from the heat and let the rice sit undisturbed with the lid on, for at least 5 minutes and for as long as 30 minutes. This lets the moisture redistribute, resulting in a more uniform texture, with the bottom layer as fluffy as the top.

stir-frying rice

For perfect fried rice, with loose separate grains, it is important to use cold cooked rice and to heat the skillet or wok until it is really hot before you add the rice. When a recipe calls for cold cooked rice, you should use rice that has been cooled quickly after it has been cooked and then stored in the refrigerator until ready to use in your recipe.

essential equipment

You will not need any expensive or complicated equipment to cook curries, but a few essential items will help you prepare them in an easy and efficient manner. You will need the basic tools that every kitchen usually has, such as ladles, spoons, strainers, colanders, cutting boards, and knives, but a few other items are worthwhile having.

grinding & blending

The secret of any good curry is the base, a mixture of a number of spices and herbs combined to form a dry curry powder or a wet curry paste. A mortar and pestle is the traditional method of combining the ingredients and is always reliable, but it does involve a lot of elbow grease.

Alternatively, you can use an electric coffee grinder for grinding dry spices. They are inexpensive and widely available, but make sure you keep one grinder just for spices, or your coffee will end up tasting fairly strange.

When you have to grind or blend together wet ingredients and dry spices to make a curry paste, a mini blender is invaluable, because it will give you a smooth mixture with ease. Most standard food processors are simply too big to handle small quantities effectively.

stove-top cooking

Choose heavy saucepans, skillets, and woks. The thick bottom will ensure the food is heated evenly, without burning or sticking to the bottom of the pan, especially when it is cooked for a long, slow period. A large saucepan with a tight-fitting lid is invaluable.

Even with a heavy saucepan, a heat diffuser is useful for gentle cooking. This is a disk made from perforated metal, usually with a removable handle, that sits on top of the heat source. You place your pan on top, and it is especially useful when an even, low, well-distributed heat is required, for example, for slow-cooking curries and for perfectly cooked

rice. Inexpensive heat diffusers are widely available from good kitchen stores and they will last you for years.

curry powders & pastes

Most curry recipes call for a curry powder or paste. Many of the recipes in this book give directions for making one, while others use a standard curry powder or a common paste such as Thai green curry paste.

While store-bought powders and pastes are available, and many are good, making your own will turn a good curry into something sublime. Make a big batch when you have the time, and store dry powders in airtight jars in the refrigerator and fresh pastes in the freezer to make several beautiful curries in the weeks to come.

basic curry powder
Makes about 1 ¼ cups

2 tablespoons **ground coriander**
2 teaspoons **ground turmeric**
½ teaspoon **black mustard seeds**
¼ teaspoon **fenugreek seeds**
6–8 dried **curry leaves**
2 tablespoons **cumin seeds**
1 teaspoon **black peppercorns**
1–6 dried **red chiles**, coarsely broken
1 teaspoon **cardamom seeds**
1 **cinnamon** or **cassia bark stick**
5–6 **cloves**
¼ teaspoon **ground ginger**

For a mild curry powder, use 1–2 dried red chiles; for a medium curry powder, use 3–4; and for a hot curry powder use 5–6 chiles. Dry-roast all the ingredients in a nonstick skillet over low heat for 2–3 minutes, until fragrant. Remove from the heat and let cool. Transfer the contents of the skillet into a mini blender or clean electric coffee grinder and grind to a fine powder. Store in an airtight container for up to one month, or in the refrigerator for up to three months.

thai green curry paste
Makes ⅓–¾ cup

2 teaspoons **ground coriander**
2 teaspoons **ground cumin**
1 teaspoon **white peppercorns**
4–6 fresh **long green chiles**, chopped
4 **shallots**, finely chopped
2 tablespoons chopped **garlic**
2 teaspoons finely chopped **kaffir lime leaves**
2 tablespoons chopped **lemon grass** (tough outer leaves removed)
1 tablespoon peeled and finely chopped **galangal** or **fresh ginger root**
2 teaspoons **shrimp paste**
1 tablespoon **peanut oil**

Grind all the ingredients to a smooth paste with a mortar and pestle or mini blender. Store in an airtight container in the refrigerator for up to one month, or freeze in small portions to use as needed.

thai red curry paste
Makes ⅓ cup

2 teaspoons **ground coriander**
1 teaspoon **ground cumin**
1 teaspoon **white peppercorns**
8 dried long **red chiles**, seeded and finely chopped
2 tablespoons finely grated **garlic**
2 tablespoons finely chopped **lemon grass** (tough outer leaves removed)
1 tablespoon peeled and finely chopped **galangal or fresh ginger root**
3 fresh **cilantro roots**, finely chopped
2 teaspoons finely chopped **kaffir lime leaves**
2 teaspoons **shrimp paste**
2 tablespoons **peanut oil**

Grind all the ingredients to a smooth paste with a mortar and pestle or mini blender. Store in an airtight container in the refrigerator for up to one month, or freeze in small portions to use as needed.

appetizers & snacks

spicy potato & apple salad

Serves **4**
Preparation time **20 minutes**,
   plus chilling

1 tablespoon freshly crushed
   black pepper
1 tablespoon **cumin seeds**,
   dry-roasted and coarsely
   ground
3 teaspoons **amchoor**
1 teaspoon **chili powder**
2 **red apples**
3 **red-skinned** or **white round
   potatoes**, peeled, boiled,
   and diced
1 small **cucumber**, diced
juice of 2 **limes**
handful of chopped **cilantro**
   and **mint**
salt and **black pepper**

Mix together the four spices and set aside.

Core the apples and cut the flesh into small cubes.
Put in a bowl with the potatoes, cucumber, and lime
juice, sprinkle with the spice mixture, season, and toss
to mix well.

Cover the bowl and marinate in the refrigerator for
30 minutes to let the flavors develop. Just before
serving, toss in the herbs. Mix well and serve
immediately.

**For potato & apple salad with spiced creamy
dressing**, place 1 diced green chile, 2 crushed garlic
cloves, the juice of 2 limes, 1 teaspoon agave syrup,
1 tablespoon mild curry powder, ¼ teaspoon turmeric,
and 1¼ cups fat-free plain yogurt in a food processor
and blend until smooth. Place 3 peeled, boiled, and
diced red-skinned or white potatoes in a salad bowl
with 2 diced apples, ½ sliced red onion, and ½ sliced
cucumber. Drizzle over the dressing, toss to mix well,
and serve.

green masala chicken kebabs

Serves **4**
Preparation time **10 minutes**,
  plus marinating
Cooking time **10 minutes**

4 skinless **chicken breasts**,
  cubed
juice of **1 lime**
½ cup **fat-free plain yogurt**
1 teaspoon peeled and finely
  grated **fresh ginger root**
1 **garlic clove**, crushed
1 **fresh green chile**, seeded
  and chopped
large handful of finely chopped
  cilantro leaves
large handful of finely chopped
  mint leaves
1 tablespoon **medium curry
  powder** (see page 18)
pinch of **salt**
lime wedges, to serve

Put the chicken in a large bowl. Place all the remaining ingredients in a food processor and blend until smooth, adding a little water, if necessary. Pour the marinade over the chicken and toss to mix well. Cover and let marinate in the refrigerator overnight.

Preheat the broiler until hot. Thread the chicken onto 8 metal skewers and broil for 6–8 minutes, turning once or twice, until the chicken is cooked through. Serve immediately with lime wedges for squeezing.

For red masala chicken kebabs, mix ¼ cup fat-free plain yogurt with ¼ cup tomato paste, 1 teaspoon grated ginger, 4 crushed garlic cloves, 1 tablespoon chili powder, 1 teaspoon ground cumin, and 1 teaspoon turmeric. Pour the marinade over the chicken and marinate and cook as above.

coconut, carrot & spinach salad

Serves **4**
Preparation time **10 minutes**
Cooking time **1 minute**

5 cups finely chopped
   baby spinach
1 **carrot**, shredded
$1/3$ cup grated **fresh coconut**
2 tablespoons **peanut oil**
2 teaspoons **black mustard**
   seeds
1 teaspoon **cumin seeds**
juice of **1 lime**
juice of **1 orange**
salt and **black pepper**

Put the spinach in a large bowl with the carrot and coconut and toss together lightly.

Heat the oil a small skillet over medium heat. Add the mustard and cumin seeds, and stir-fry for 20–30 seconds, until fragrant and the mustard seeds start to "pop."

Remove from the heat and pour the flavored oil over the salad with the lime and orange juice. Season well and toss before serving.

For spicy coconut, carrot & spinach sauté, heat 1 tablespoon peanut oil in a large wok or skillet and add 1 finely diced red chile, 2 finely chopped garlic cloves, 4 finely sliced scallions, and 1 teaspoon each of cumin and black mustard seeds. Stir-fry for 1 minute, then add 1 shredded carrot. Stir-fry for 2–3 minutes and add 7 cups whole baby spinach. Stir-fry over high heat for 2–3 minutes or until the spinach has just wilted. Season, sprinkle with $1/3$ cup grated fresh coconut, and serve immediately.

chilled tomato & yogurt soup

Serves **4**

Preparation time **5 minutes**, plus chilling

6 **tomatoes**, peeled, seeded, and chopped
2 tablespoons **lemon juice**
1 tablespoon **white wine vinegar**
1 teaspoon **mild curry powder** (see page 18)
1 cup **fat-free plain yogurt**, whisked
salt and **black pepper**
small handful of chopped **cilantro leaves**, to garnish

Put the tomatoes, lemon juice, vinegar, curry powder, and yogurt in a food processor and blend until smooth. Season well, transfer to a bowl, cover, and chill in the refrigerator for 3–4 hours or overnight.

Ladle the soup into chilled soup bowls, garnish with a sprinkling of chopped cilantro, and serve immediately.

For chilled spicy cucumber & yogurt soup, replace the tomatoes with 2 large peeled, seeded, and diced cucumbers and 4 finely sliced scallions. Blend and chill as above. To serve, sprinkle with 1 tablespoon dry-roasted cumin seeds and a small handful of chopped mint leaves.

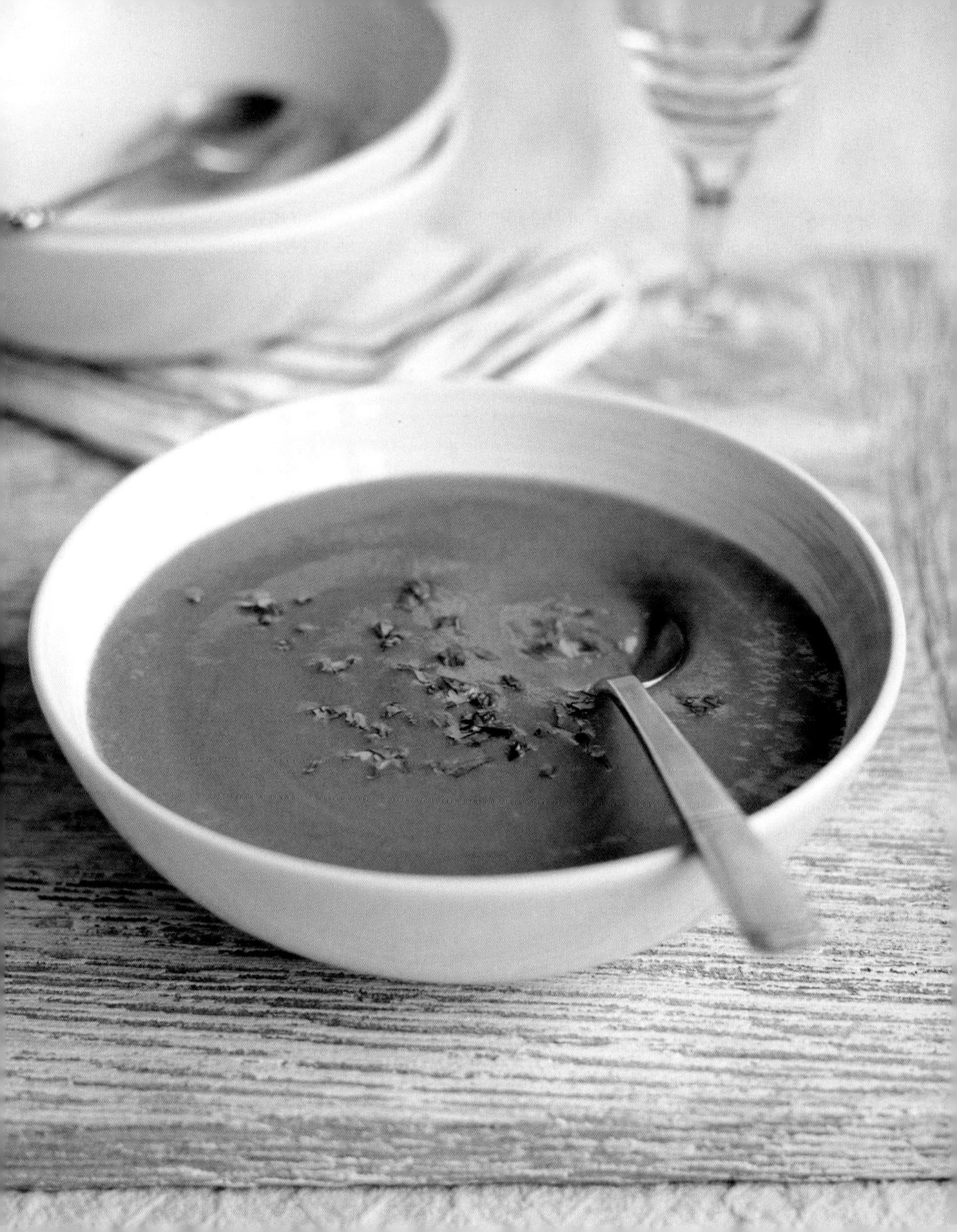

chile & jumbo shrimp salad

Serves **4**
Preparation time **10 minutes**
Cooking time **3–4 minutes**

1 teaspoon **sesame oil**
8 oz **raw jumbo shrimp**,
   peeled and deveined
4 **scallions**, thinly sliced on
   the diagonal
4 inch piece of **cucumber**,
   seeded and cut into
   matchsticks
16 **cherry tomatoes**, halved
1 tablespoon finely chopped
   cilantro leaves
1 teaspoon **Thai fish sauce**
2 **fresh red chiles**, finely
   chopped
¼ cup **lemon juice**

Heat the oil in a large wok or skillet over medium-high heat. When the oil is hot, add the shrimp and stir-fry for 3–4 minutes, until they turn pink.

Remove the shrimp from the pan with a slotted spoon, and cut into thin slices on the diagonal. Put them in a bowl with the remaining ingredients and toss to mix well. Serve immediately.

For spicy chicken & chile salad, mix ⅓ cup lemon juice with ¼ cup sweet chili sauce, 2 tablespoons light soy sauce, 1 finely diced red chile, and 1 teaspoon sesame oil. Place 3 shredded, cooked chicken breasts in a wide bowl and add 6 thinly sliced scallions, 16 halved cherry tomatoes, ½ sliced cucumber, and a large handful of cilantro leaves. Spoon the dressing over the salad, toss to mix well, and serve.

pork, potato & pea samosas

Makes **20**
Preparation time **20 minutes**,
   plus chilling
Cooking time **25 minutes**

1 tablespoon **peanut oil**
10 oz **ground pork**
1 **onion**, chopped
1 tablespoon **medium curry
   powder** (see page 16)
1 small **russet potato**, peeled,
   boiled, and finely diced
1/3 cup **frozen peas**
1/4 cup chopped **cilantro
   leaves**
1/4 cup chopped **mint leaves**
5 **phyllo pastry sheets**, each
   10 x 20 inches
1 **egg**, beaten
cooking oil spray
salt and **black pepper**

Heat the oil in a skillet over medium heat. Add the pork, onion, and curry powder, season, and cook for about 10 minutes, until the pork is just cooked and the juices have evaporated from the pan. Add the potato and peas and mix well. Remove the pan from the heat, add the chopped herbs, and set aside to cool.

Lay the phyllo pastry sheets in a stack on a clean board. Cut into quarters to make four rectangles from each sheet. Cover the pastry with a barely damp dish towel to prevent it from drying out.

Lay one sheet of phyllo on the work surface with a short side nearest you. Place 2 teaspoons of the filling on the end nearest you and fold the bottom right corner of the pastry over to meet the left-hand side and enclose the filling in a triangle. Continue folding the package over down the length of the pastry to make a neat triangular package. Brush the loose edge with a little of the beaten egg to seal, then put on a baking sheet. Repeat to make 20 samosas, then brush them with beaten egg and chill until ready to cook.

Preheat the oven to 425°F. Lightly spray the samosas with cooking oil spray and cook in the preheated oven for 12–15 minutes, until golden brown. Serve warm.

For mint & yogurt chutney, to serve as an accompaniment, place a large handful of chopped mint leaves in a blender with a small handful of chopped cilantro leaves, 1 finely chopped green chile, 2 chopped garlic cloves, 1 teaspoon grated ginger root, the juice of 2 limes, 2 teaspoons agave syrup, and 1 cup fat-free plain yogurt. Season and blend until smooth.

mint, spinach & buttermilk shorba

Serves **4**
Preparation time **10 minutes**

1²/₃ cups **frozen spinach**,
   defrosted
1 **garlic clove**, crushed
1 teaspoon **mild curry
   powder** (see page 16)
½ teaspoon peeled and finely
   grated **fresh ginger root**
2 cups **buttermilk**
¹/₃ cup finely chopped **mint
   leaves**, plus extra to garnish
1½ cups **iced water**
8 **ice cubes**
salt and **black pepper**

Put the spinach in a colander and squeeze out the excess water. Chop the spinach finely.

Transfer to a food processor with the garlic, curry powder, ginger, and buttermilk. Season well and stir in the chopped mint. Add the measured water and process the mixture until smooth.

Ladle the soup into chilled bowls, drop 2 ice cubes into each bowl, and garnish with a few extra mint leaves. Serve immediately.

For curried spinach & potato soup, place 6 cups finely chopped spinach in a saucepan with 1 finely chopped onion, 2 crushed garlic cloves, 1 teaspoon finely grated ginger, 1 finely chopped red chile, 1 teaspoon mild curry powder (see page 16), and 4 cups vegetable stock. Bring to a boil. Peel 2 red-skinned or white round potatoes, cut into ¾ inch dice, and add to the spinach mixture. Bring back to a boil, reduce the heat, and simmer for 15–20 minutes or until the potato is tender. Season and serve in warmed bowls.

peanut & cucumber salad

Serves **4**
Preparation time **5 minutes**
Cooking time **5 minutes**

1 large **cucumber**, peeled and
   finely chopped
¼ cup **lemon juice**
1 tablespoon **light olive oil**
1 teaspoon **yellow mustard
   seeds**
2 teaspoons **black mustard
   seeds**
8–10 **curry leaves**
1–2 **fresh red chiles**, seeded
   and finely chopped
¼ cup finely chopped **roasted
   peanuts**
salt and **black pepper**

Put the cucumber in a large bowl, sprinkle with the lemon juice, and season with salt. Stir to mix well and set aside.

Heat the oil in a small skillet over medium heat. Add the mustard seeds, curry leaves, and chile, and stir-fry for 1–2 minutes, until fragrant and the mustard seeds start to "pop."

Add the contents of the skillet to the cucumber mixture. Toss to mix well, sprinkle over the chopped peanuts, and serve immediately.

For spicy roasted tomato salad, cut 10 plum tomatoes in half and place on a baking sheet, cut side up. Season and sprinkle with 1 tablespoon mild curry powder (see page 16) and 2 teaspoons cumin seeds. Lightly spray with cooking oil spray and roast in a preheated oven, at 400°F, for 12–15 minutes. Let cool. Arrange 7 cups mixed salad greens on a wide serving plate with ½ sliced red onion. Arrange the cooled tomatoes over the salad, squeeze with the juice of 2 limes, and sprinkle with ¼ cup toasted pumpkin seeds.

hara boti kebabs

Serves **4**

Preparation time **20 minutes**, plus marinating

Cooking time **12–15 minutes**

1½ lb **lean leg of lamb**, cubed

1 **onion**, finely chopped

2 teaspoons **garlic salt**

2 teaspoons **ground ginger**

1 tablespoon **ground cumin**

1 tablespoon **mild curry powder** (see page 16)

1 tablespoon **mild chili powder**

1 tablespoon **fennel seeds**

⅓ cup finely chopped **cilantro leaves**

2 tablespoons finely chopped **mint leaves**

1 cup **fat-free plain yogurt**

½ teaspoon **agave syrup**

juice of 2 **limes**

salt and **black pepper**

Put the lamb in a large nonmetallic dish. Place all the remaining ingredients in a food processor and blend until smooth. Season well and pour the marinade over the lamb. Cover and marinate in the refrigerator for 24–48 hours.

Remove the lamb from the refrigerator and let come to room temperature. Preheat the oven to 400°F.

Thread the lamb onto 8–12 metal skewers, and arrange on a baking sheet lined with parchment paper. Cook in the preheated oven for 12–15 minutes, until tender and cooked through.

For cumin, chile & lemon rice, to serve as an accompaniment, place 2 teaspoons cumin seeds in a saucepan with 1 diced red chile, 1 teaspoon ground turmeric, the finely grated rind and juice of 1 lemon, 1½ cups basmati or other long-grain rice, and 2¾ cups hot vegetable stock. Season and bring to a boil. Reduce the heat to low, cover the pan, and cook gently for 10–12 minutes or according to the package directions, until all the liquid has been absorbed. Remove from the heat and let stand, covered and undisturbed, for 10–15 minutes. Fluff up the grains with a fork and serve.

carrot & red cabbage slaw

Serves **4**

Preparation time **10 minutes**

Cooking time **1 minute**

3 large **carrots**, shredded

3 cups finely shredded
   red cabbage

juice of 2 **limes**

2 teaspoons **agave syrup**

2 tablespoons **light olive oil**

1 fresh **red chile,** finely diced

1 tablespoon **black mustard
   seeds**

salt and **black pepper**

Put the carrots and red cabbage in a large bowl. Mix together the lime juice and agave syrup, and stir into the vegetables. Toss to mix well and set aside.

Heat the oil in a small skillet over medium heat. Add the chile and mustard seeds, and stir-fry for 20–30 seconds, until fragrant and the mustard seeds start to "pop."

Scrape the contents of the skillet over the salad, season well, and toss to combine. Serve immediately.

For toasted spiced chapati wedges, to serve as an accompaniment, cut 4 store-bought chapatis (available in Asian grocery stores), flour tortillas, or pita breads into wedges and arrange on 2 large baking sheets. Lightly spray with cooking oil spray and sprinkle with 1 tablespoon crushed cumin seeds, 1 tablespoon nigella seeds, 2 teaspoons mild chili powder, and a little sea salt. Cook in a preheated oven, at 350°F, for 8–10 minutes or until crisp. Serve hot.

chile-seared squid & herb salad

Serves **4**
Preparation time **15 minutes**,
   plus marinating
Cooking time **10 minutes**

large pinch of **sea salt**
1 teaspoon **ground coriander**
1 teaspoon **ground cumin**
1 teaspoon **hot chili powder**
½ cup **lemon juice**
1 teaspoon **tomato paste**
1 **fresh red chile,** seeded and
   finely sliced
1 teaspoon peeled and finely
   grated **fresh ginger root**
1 **garlic clove,** crushed
1½ lb **squid,** cut into bite-size
   pieces
1 small **red onion,** thinly sliced
large handful of chopped
   cilantro leaves
small handful of chopped
   mint leaves

Mix the salt, ground spices, chili powder, lemon juice, tomato paste, chile, ginger, and garlic in a large bowl and add the squid. Toss to coat evenly, cover, and let stand at room temperature for 15 minutes.

Heat a nonstick, ridged grill pan over high heat. Working in batches, lift the squid from the marinade and sear in the hot pan for 1–2 minutes, then remove from the pan and keep warm while you cook the remaining squid.

Add the red onion and herbs to the cooked squid, toss to mix well, and serve immediately.

For jumbo shrimp, mango & herb salad, replace the squid with 1½ lb raw, peeled jumbo shrimp. Marinate in the spice mixture for 10 minutes, then cook in the smoking hot pan in batches for 2–3 minutes on each side, or until pink and cooked through. Transfer to a wide salad bowl and stir in a large handful each of cilantro and mint leaves and the diced flesh of 1 ripe mango. Toss to mix well and serve

spicy zucchini fritters

Serves **4**

Preparation time **15 minutes**,
   plus draining

Cooking time **10–15 minutes**

3 **zucchini**

2 large **scallions**, grated

1 **garlic clove**, finely chopped

finely grated rind of 1 **lemon**

¼ cup **chickpea (besan) flour**

2 teaspoons **medium curry
   powder** (see page 16)

1 **fresh red chile,** seeded and
   finely chopped

2 tablespoons finely chopped
   mint leaves

2 tablespoons finely chopped
   cilantro leaves

2 **eggs**, lightly beaten

2 tablespoons **light olive oil**

salt and **black pepper**

Shred the zucchini into a colander. Sprinkle lightly with salt and let stand for at least 1 hour to drain. Squeeze out the remaining liquid.

Put the remaining ingredients, except the eggs and olive oil, in a mixing bowl and add the zucchini. Season lightly, keeping in mind you have already salted the zucchini, and mix well. Add the eggs and mix again to combine.

Heat half the olive oil in a large skillet over medium-high heat. Place tablespoons of the mixture, well spaced apart, in the pan and press down with the back of the spoon. Cook for 1–2 minutes on each side, until golden and cooked through. Remove from the pan and keep warm. Repeat to cook the rest of the fritters in the same way, adding the remaining oil to the pan when necessary.

For cucumber, mango & fromage blanc relish, to serve as an accompaniment, peel, seed, and coarsely grate 1 cucumber into a fine mesh strainer. Squeeze out any excess liquid using the back of a spoon. Put the grated cucumber in a bowl with 2 tablespoons hot mango chutney and 1 cup fat-free fromage blanc or Greek yogurt. Stir in a small handful of finely chopped cilantro leaves, season, and chill until required.

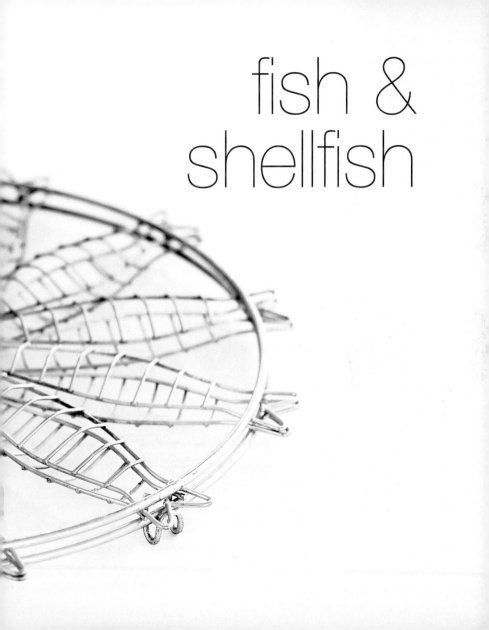

fish &
shellfish

cambodian fish curry

Serves **4**
Preparation time **10 minutes**
Cooking time **15 minutes**

2 tablespoons finely chopped
 lemon grass (tough outer
 leaves removed)
1 tablespoon peeled and finely
 chopped **galangal** or **ginger**
3 **fresh red chiles**, coarsely
 chopped
4 **garlic cloves**, coarsely
 chopped
1 cup **water**
1½ lb thick **halibut fillet**,
 skinned and cubed
1 tablespoon **peanut oil**
1 cup **coconut milk**
1 tablespoon **Thai fish sauce**
2 tablespoons chopped **dry-
 roasted peanuts**
small handful of **Thai basil
 leaves**

Put the lemon grass, galangal, chiles, and garlic in a
mini blender with the measured water and blend to a
smooth paste. Set aside.

Pat the fish dry with paper towels, arrange on a
broiler rack and cook under a medium-hot broiler
for 10–12 minutes or until cooked through.

Meanwhile, heat the oil in a nonstick skillet and stir-fry
the spice paste for 4–5 minutes. Add the coconut milk
and fish sauce and cook, stirring, over high heat for
5 minutes. Add the fish to the pan with the peanuts and
basil, and toss gently to mix well. Serve immediately.

For spicy fish with lemon grass & coconut, put
4 thick cod fillets in a shallow, lightly greased ovenproof
dish in a single layer. Mix together 2 tablespoons finely
chopped lemon grass, 2 finely chopped fresh red chiles,
2 teaspoons each of grated fresh ginger root and garlic,
and ½ cup coconut milk. Season and spoon the sauce
over the fish. Cook in a preheated oven, at 350°F,
for 15–20 minutes or until cooked through. Serve
garnished with chopped cilantro.

dry shrimp curry

Serves **4**
Preparation time **10 minutes**
Cooking time **10 minutes**

1 **onion**, coarsely chopped
4 **garlic cloves**, chopped
½ cup **lemon juice**
1 teaspoon peeled and finely
    grated **fresh ginger root**
1 teaspoon **ground turmeric**
½ teaspoon **chili powder**
2 teaspoons **store-bought
    medium curry paste**
1 tablespoon **peanut oil**
1 lb **raw jumbo shrimp**,
    peeled and deveined
¼ cup chopped **cilantro
    leaves**
4 **scallions**, finely sliced
salt

Put the onion, garlic, lemon juice, ginger, turmeric, chili powder, and curry paste in a food processor and blend until fairly smooth. Season with salt.

Heat the oil in a wide saucepan over medium heat. Add the onion paste and stir-fry for 2–3 minutes. Add the shrimp and stir-fry for another 4–5 minutes, until they turn pink and are cooked through.

Remove from the heat and stir in the cilantro and scallions. Serve immediately.

For lemon & herbed couscous, to serve as an accompaniment, place 1½ cups couscous in a shallow heatproof bowl. Add boiling water to just cover the couscous, cover tightly, and let stand for 12–15 minutes or according to the package directions. Fluff up the grains of the couscous with a fork, season, and stir in a large handful each of chopped cilantro and mint. Squeeze the juice of 1 lemon over the couscous and serve immediately.

thai mussel curry with ginger

Serves **4**
Preparation time **30 minutes**
Cooking time **15 minutes**

½–1 **fresh red chile**
2 **shallots**, quartered
1 **lemon grass stalk**
1 tablespoon peeled and finely
    chopped **fresh ginger root**
1 tablespoon **peanut oil**
1¾ cups **coconut milk**
4–5 **kaffir lime leaves**
⅔ cup **fish stock**
2 teaspoons **Thai fish sauce**
3 lb **mussels**, scrubbed and
    debearded
small bunch of **cilantro**, torn
    into pieces, to garnish

Put the chile, shallots, lemon grass, and ginger into a mini blender and blend until finely chopped.

Heat the oil in large, deep saucepan, add the finely chopped ingredients, and sauté over medium heat for 5 minutes, stirring until softened. Add the coconut milk, lime leaves, fish stock, and fish sauce and cook for 3 minutes.

Add the mussels, cover the pan, and cook for about 5 minutes or until the mussel shells have opened, discarding any that do not open. Spoon into warmed bowls and serve garnished with cilantro.

For Thai chicken & eggplant curry, prepare the above recipe up to the end of the second step, replacing the fish stock with 1 cup chicken stock. Stir in 1 diced eggplant and 2 skinless, boneless chicken breasts, cut into large chunks. Bring back to a boil, cover, and simmer for 12–15 minutes or until the chicken is cooked and the eggplant tender. Serve sprinkled with cilantro.

cochin fish curry

Serves **4**
Preparation time **15 minutes**
Cooking time **30–35 minutes**

1 **onion**, chopped
4 **garlic cloves**, crushed
2 **fresh green chiles**, seeded and chopped
1 tablespoon **ground cumin**
1 teaspoon **ground coriander**
1 teaspoon **ground turmeric**
small handful of finely chopped **cilantro leaves**, plus extra to garnish
1 cup **water**
1 tablespoon **peanut oil**
6 **curry leaves**
1¾ cups **coconut milk**
1¾ lb thick **cod** or **halibut fillet**, skinned and cubed
salt and **black pepper**

Put the onion, garlic, chiles, cumin, ground coriander, turmeric, cilantro leaves, and measured water in a food processor and blend to a smooth paste.

Heat the oil in a large skillet over high heat. Add the curry leaves and stir-fry for 20–30 seconds. Now add the blended paste and cook, stirring, over high heat for 3–4 minutes, until fragrant. Reduce the heat, pour in the coconut milk, and simmer gently, uncovered, for 20 minutes.

Add the fish to the pan in a single layer and bring back to a boil. Reduce the heat and simmer gently for 5–6 minutes, until the fish is just cooked through. Season and remove from the heat. Garnish with cilantro leaves and serve with steamed basmati rice.

For creamy shrimp & zucchini curry, replace the fish with 1½ lb raw, peeled jumbo shrimp and 2 zucchini, cut into ½ x 1½ inch batons. Cook as above, until the shrimp turn pink and are cooked through and the zucchini is just tender. Serve with steamed basmati rice.

curried crab & shrimp cakes

Serves **4**
Preparation time **10 minutes**,
   plus chilling
Cooking time **20–25 minutes**

13 oz **fresh white crabmeat**
13 oz **raw jumbo shrimp**,
   peeled and deveined
1 tablespoon **hot curry
   powder** (see page 16)
2 **garlic cloves**, crushed
1 teaspoon peeled and grated
   fresh ginger root
1 **fresh red chile,** seeded and
   finely chopped
¼ cup finely chopped **red
   onion**
½ cup chopped **cilantro
   leaves**, plus extra to garnish
1 **medium egg**, beaten
2 cups **fresh whole wheat
   bread crumbs**
cooking oil spray
salt and **black pepper**
lemon wedges, to serve

Put the crabmeat, shrimp, curry powder, garlic, ginger, chile, onion, cilantro, egg, and bread crumbs in a food processor. Season well and pulse for a few seconds, until well mixed. Transfer to a bowl, cover, and chill in the refrigerator for 5–6 hours or overnight.

Preheat the oven to 400°F, line a baking sheet with parchment paper, and spray with a little cooking oil spray.

Divide the crab mixture into 16 equal portions and shape each into a round cake. Arrange on the prepared baking sheet, spray with a little cooking oil spray, and bake for 20–25 minutes, until lightly browned and cooked through. Garnish with cilantro and serve immediately with lemon wedges.

For piquant crab, shrimp & rice salad, put 13 oz each of fresh white crabmeat and cooked, peeled shrimp in a salad bowl with 2 cups cold cooked basmati rice. Add 6 finely sliced scallions, ½ finely diced cucumber, 10 halved cherry tomatoes, and a small handful of chopped cilantro leaves. In a small bowl, whisk 3 tablespoons light olive oil with ¼ cup lemon juice, 1 teaspoon agave syrup, and 1 finely chopped red chile. Season, pour the dressing over the salad, and toss to mix well.

monkfish korma

Serves **4**
Preparation time **10 minutes**
Cooking time **20 minutes**

1 tablespoon **peanut oil**
2 tablespoons **korma curry powder**
1½ lb **monkfish fillet**, cubed
large bunch of **cilantro leaves**, finely chopped
1 **red onion**, finely chopped
finely grated rind and juice of 2 **limes**
1¾ cups **coconut milk**
salt and **black pepper**

Heat the oil in a wide saucepan over medium heat. Add the curry powder and stir-fry for 20–30 seconds or until fragrant. Add the monkfish, cilantro, and red onion and cook, stirring, for another 20–30 seconds.

Add the lime rind and juice and the coconut milk. Bring to a boil, reduce the heat, and simmer for 15 minutes or until the fish is cooked through. Season to taste and serve immediately with steamed rice.

For monkfish Madras, replace the korma curry powder with Madras curry powder, and the coconut milk with 1 cup tomato puree or sauce and 1 cup fish stock. Cook as above until the fish is cooked through. Serve with warmed naan, chapatis, or pita breads.

red fish, broccoli & bean curry

Serves **4**
Preparation time **15 minutes**
Cooking time **10 minutes**

1 tablespoon **peanut oil**
1½–2 tablespoons **Thai red curry paste** (see page 17)
1 cup **coconut milk**
1 cup **vegetable stock**
1 tablespoon **tamarind paste**
1 tablespoon **Thai fish sauce**
1 tablespoon **palm sugar** or **brown sugar**
3 cups **broccoli florets**
2 cups 1-inch **green bean** pieces
1 pound thick **white fish fillet**, skinned and cubed
1 cup drained canned **bamboo shoots** (optional)
small handful of **Thai basil leaves**, to garnish
lime wedges, to serve

Heat the oil in a large wok or skillet over medium heat, add the curry paste, and stir-fry for 1–2 minutes. Stir in the coconut milk, stock, tamarind paste, fish sauce, and sugar and bring to a boil, then reduce the heat and simmer gently for another 2–3 minutes.

Add the broccoli and beans and simmer gently for 2 minutes. Stir in the fish and simmer gently for another 3–4 minutes or until just cooked through. Stir in the bamboo shoots, if using.

Ladle into warmed bowls, sprinkle with Thai basil, and serve with lime wedges.

For Thai mixed seafood curry, replace the broccoli and green beans with 1 large thinly sliced carrot and 1 thinly sliced red bell pepper. Follow the recipe above, omitting the fish, but adding 12 raw jumbo shrimp, peeled and deveined, 4 oz prepared squid rings, and 1 lb scrubbed and debearded mussels. Simmer gently until the mussels open, discarding any that do not. Add 1 cup fresh or canned pineapple chunks instead of the bamboo shoots and serve as above.

sweet & sour salmon curry

Serves **4**
Preparation time **15 minutes**
Cooking time **20 minutes**

1 tablespoon **Thai fish sauce**
1 teaspoon **palm sugar** or
   brown sugar
2 **lemon grass stalks**, bruised
2½ cups **water**
2 tablespoons **lemon juice**
1 tablespoon **tamarind paste**
1 cup **pineapple chunks**
4 **salmon fillets**, about 7 oz
   each, skinned

Curry paste
2 **garlic cloves**, peeled
5 **dried red chiles**
large pinch of **sea salt**
1 teaspoon **ground turmeric**
2 tablespoons finely chopped
   lemon grass (tough outer
   leaves removed)
1 tablespoon **shrimp paste**

Put all the ingredients for the curry paste in a mini blender and blend until smooth, adding a little water, if necessary. Transfer the paste to a wide saucepan and add the fish sauce, sugar, lemon grass stalks, and two-thirds of the measured water. Bring to a boil, reduce the heat, and simmer for 8–10 minutes.

Mix the lemon juice with the tamarind paste and remaining water. Add to the saucepan with the pineapple and stir to mix well. Add the salmon fillets and simmer gently for 8–10 minutes, until cooked through. Remove from the heat and serve immediately with steamed jasmine rice.

For quick Thai red cod curry, lightly spray a large skillet with cooking oil spray and stir-fry 2 finely chopped garlic cloves, 4 finely sliced shallots, 2 teaspoons grated fresh ginger root, and 2 tablespoons Thai red curry paste (see page 17) for 2–3 minutes. Add 1¾ cups coconut milk, 1 teaspoon agave syrup, and 1 cup fish stock and bring to a boil. Add 1½ lb cubed cod fillet and cook for 5–6 minutes or until cooked through. Remove from the heat and serve immediately with steamed jasmine rice.

curry leaf & tomato shrimp

Serves **4**
Preparation time **15 minutes**
Cooking time **15–20 minutes**

1 tablespoon **peanut oil**
10–12 **curry leaves**
2 **large shallots**, halved and
   finely sliced
2 teaspoons finely grated
   garlic
1 teaspoon peeled and finely
   grated **fresh ginger root**
1 tablespoon **fennel seeds**
1 tablespoon **medium curry
   powder** (see page 16)
6 **large ripe tomatoes**,
   peeled, seeded and chopped
1½ lb **raw jumbo shrimp**,
   peeled and deveined
salt

Heat the oil in a large wok or skillet over medium heat. Add the curry leaves and stir-fry for 30 seconds. Add the shallots and stir-fry for another 4–5 minutes.

Add the garlic, ginger, and fennel seeds, reduce the heat, and cook gently for 2–3 minutes. Sprinkle with the curry powder and add the tomatoes, including any juices. Increase the heat and stir-fry for 3–4 minutes.

Add the shrimp and continue cooking over high heat for 6–7 minutes, until the shrimp turn pink and are just cooked through. Remove from the heat, season to taste, and serve immediately with rice or crushed sesame spiced potatoes.

For crushed sesame spiced potatoes, to serve as an accompaniment, peel 4 red-skinned or white round potatoes and cut into ½ inch dice. Boil for 12 minutes or until just tender, then drain thoroughly. Heat 1 tablespoon peanut oil in a large skillet over high heat. Add 1 tablespoon sesame seeds, 2 teaspoons cumin seeds, 2 teaspoons red chili powder, ¼ teaspoon ground turmeric, and the potatoes and stir-fry for 6–8 minutes, crushing them lightly with the back of a spoon. Season and serve.

monkfish tikka kebabs

Serves **4**
Preparation time **15 minutes**,
 plus marinating
Cooking time **8–10 minutes**

1½ lb **monkfish fillet**, cubed
2 **red bell peppers**, cored,
 seeded, and cubed
2 **yellow bell peppers**, cored,
 seeded, and cubed
salt and **black pepper**
chopped **cilantro** and **mint
 leaves**, to garnish
lime wedges, to serve

Tikka marinade
1½ cups **fat-free plain yogurt**
2 tablespoons finely grated
 onion
1 tablespoon finely grated
 garlic
1 tablespoon peeled and finely
 grated **fresh ginger root**
juice of 2 **limes**
3 tablespoons **tikka curry
 powder**

Mix all the marinade ingredients in a large bowl.
Add the fish and bell peppers, season well, and toss
to coat evenly. Cover and marinate in the refrigerator
for 1–2 hours.

Preheat a broiler or barbecue grill until hot. Thread the
fish and bell peppers onto 8 metal skewers and cook for
4–5 minutes on each side until the fish is just cooked
through. Serve immediately, garnished with chopped
cilantro and mint, with lime wedges for squeezing.

For monkfish tikka wraps, cook the fish and
bell peppers as above and remove from the skewers.
Warm 8 medium chapatis or flour tortillas and top each
one with a small handful of shredded lettuce. Divide
the fish and bell peppers among them, drizzle each
with a little fat-free fromage blanc or Greek yogurt,
wrap up, and serve.

simple fish & potato curry

Serves **4**
Preparation time **20 minutes**
Cooking time **40 minutes**

$^1/_3$ cup peeled and grated
   fresh **ginger root**
1 teaspoon **ground turmeric**
2 **garlic cloves**, crushed
2 teaspoons **medium curry
   paste**
$^2/_3$ cup **fat-free plain yogurt**
1$^1/_4$ lb **white fish fillet**, skinned
   and cubed
2 tablespoons **peanut oil**
1 large **onion**, sliced
1 **cinnamon stick**, halved
2 teaspoons **palm sugar** or
   brown sugar
2 **bay leaves**
1 (14$^1/_2$ oz) can **diced
   tomatoes**
1$^1/_4$ cups **fish stock**
4 **red-skinned** or **white round
   potatoes**, cubed
small handful of chopped
   cilantro leaves
salt and **black pepper**

Mix the ginger with the turmeric, garlic, and curry paste in a large bowl. Stir in the yogurt until well combined, then add the fish and toss to coat in the spice mixture.

Heat the oil in a large saucepan and gently sauté the onion, cinnamon, sugar, and bay leaves until the onion is soft. Add the tomatoes, stock, and potatoes and bring to a boil. Cook, uncovered, for about 20 minutes, until the potatoes are tender and the sauce has thickened.

Add the fish and spicy yogurt and reduce the heat to its lowest setting. Cook gently for about 10 minutes or until the fish is cooked through. Season to taste and stir in the cilantro before serving.

For homemade fish stock, melt a pat of butter in a large saucepan and gently sauté 2 coarsely chopped shallots, 1 small coarsely chopped leek, and 1 coarsely chopped celery stick or fennel bulb. Add 2 lb white fish bones, heads, and trimmings, or shrimp shells, several parsley sprigs, $^1/_2$ lemon, and 1 teaspoon peppercorns. Cover with cold water and bring to a simmer. Cook, uncovered, on the lowest setting for 30 minutes. Strain through a strainer and let cool.

singapore curried scallops

Serves **4**
Preparation time **10 minutes**
Cooking time **5 minutes**

24 fresh **scallops**
3 tablespoons **mild curry
  powder** (see page 16)
1 tablespoon **peanut oil**
¼ cup **light soy sauce**
2 tablespoons **rice wine**
2 **fresh red chiles**, finely
  sliced
3 inch piece of **fresh ginger
  root**, peeled and finely
  shredded
6 **scallions**, finely sliced
salt and **black pepper**

Put the scallops on a plate, dust the curry powder over them, and lightly season to taste. Toss to mix well.

Heat the oil in a large nonstick skillet. When it is hot, add the scallops, spacing them out around the pan. Sear for 1–2 minutes on each side, then remove from the pan and arrange on a warmed serving plate.

Mix together the soy sauce and wine and sprinkle it over the scallops. Sprinkle a little chile, ginger, and scallion over each scallop, and serve immediately with egg-fried rice.

For mild scallop & coconut curry, heat 1 tablespoon peanut oil in a large skillet and add 1 finely chopped onion, 1 seeded and finely chopped red chile, 2 finely chopped garlic cloves, and 1 teaspoon finely diced ginger. Stir-fry for 3–4 minutes or until the onion has just softened, then add 1 tablespoon mild curry powder (see page 16) and stir-fry for 1 minute. Add 1¾ cups coconut milk and 1 cup tomato puree or tomato sauce and bring to a boil. Reduce the heat to medium and cook for 6–8 minutes, stirring often. Season to taste, stir in 24 fresh scallops, and cook for 4–5 minutes or until the scallops are just cooked through. Remove from the heat and serve in warmed bowls with rice.

yellow salmon curry

Serves **4**
Preparation time **15 minutes**
Cooking time **25–30 minutes**

3 **garlic cloves**, finely grated
2 **fresh green chiles**, seeded
   and finely chopped
2 teaspoons peeled and finely
   grated **fresh ginger root**
1 tablespoon **peanut oil**
1 **onion**, finely chopped
1 tablespoon **ground turmeric**
1 cup **coconut milk**
1 cup **water**
2 **red-skinned** or **white round
   potatoes**, peeled and diced
4 thick **salmon steaks**, about
   7 oz each
2 **tomatoes**, coarsely chopped
salt
chopped **cilantro leaves**, to
   garnish

Pound the garlic, chiles, and ginger with a mortar and pestle until you have a smooth paste.

Heat the oil in a large, nonstick wok or saucepan over medium heat. Add the paste and stir-fry for 2–3 minutes, then add the onion and turmeric. Stir-fry for another 2–3 minutes, until fragrant.

Stir in the coconut milk, measured water, and the potatoes. Bring to a boil, reduce the heat to low, and simmer gently for 10–12 minutes, stirring occasionally.

Season the fish with salt and add to the pan with the tomatoes. Bring the mixture back to a boil and simmer gently for 6–8 minutes, until the fish is cooked through. Remove from the heat and garnish with chopped cilantro. Serve hot with steamed white rice.

For yellow mussel curry, replace the salmon with 2 lb mussels that have been scrubbed and debearded. Cover the pan and cook over high heat for 6–8 minutes or until the mussels have opened, discarding any that do not. Remove from the heat, garnish with chopped cilantro, and serve hot with crusty bread.

spicy cod & tomato curry

Serves **4**

Preparation time **15 minutes**

Cooking time **40–50 minutes**

¼ cup **lemon juice**

¼ cup **rice wine vinegar**

2 tablespoons **cumin seeds**

2 tablespoons **hot curry powder** (see page 16)

large pinch of **salt**

1½ lb thick **cod fillet**, skinned and cubed

1 tablespoon **peanut oil**

1 **onion**, finely chopped

3 **garlic cloves**, finely chopped

2 teaspoons peeled and finely grated **fresh ginger root**

2 (14½ oz) cans **diced tomatoes**

1 teaspoon **agave syrup**

Mix the lemon juice with the vinegar, cumin seeds, curry powder, and salt in a shallow nonmetallic bowl. Add the fish and turn to coat evenly. Cover and marinate in the refrigerator for 25–30 minutes.

Meanwhile, heat a wok or large skillet with a lid over high heat and add the oil. When the oil is hot, add the onion, garlic, and ginger. Reduce the heat and cook gently for 10 minutes, stirring occasionally.

Add the tomatoes and agave syrup, stir well, and bring to a boil. Reduce the heat, cover, and cook gently for 15–20 minutes, stirring occasionally.

Add the fish and its marinade, and stir gently to mix. Cover and simmer gently for 15–20 minutes, until the fish is cooked through. Ladle into shallow bowls and serve with steamed basmati rice.

For cod & tomato biryani, place 1 tablespoon medium curry powder (see page 16) in a medium saucepan with 1 bay leaf, 1 cinnamon stick, a large pinch of saffron, 4 crushed cardamom pods, 3 cloves, ⅓ cup tomato paste, and 1½ cups basmati rice. Pour in 2¾ cups hot fish stock, season, and stir to mix well. Bring back to a boil and gently stir in 12 oz skinless cod fillet chunks. Reduce the heat to low, cover the pan, and cook gently for 10–12 minutes or until all the liquid has been absorbed. Remove from the heat and let stand, covered and undisturbed, for 10–15 minutes. Fluff up the grains with a fork before serving.

kerala mackerel curry

Serves **4**

Preparation time **10 minutes**,
  plus soaking

Cooking time **15–20 minutes**

4 **dried Kashmiri chiles**,
  soaked in hot water for
  30 minutes

1 tablespoon **paprika**

2 tablespoons **mild curry
  powder** (see page 16)

2 cups shredded **fresh
  coconut**

1 cup **coconut milk**

1 cup **water**

2 tablespoons **tamarind paste**

2 **fresh green chiles**, halved
  lengthwise

1 tablespoon peeled and finely
  grated **fresh ginger root**

1 small **onion**, finely chopped

1½ lb **mackerel fillets**

salt

Put the soaked chiles, paprika, curry powder, and coconut in a food processor with the coconut milk and blend to a smooth paste.

Transfer the spice paste to a wide saucepan, add the measured water, stir to mix well, and bring to a gentle simmer over medium-low heat. Add the tamarind paste, green chiles, ginger, and onion, and season to taste. Stir and simmer for 2–3 minutes.

Add the fish to the pan, stir once, cover, and simmer gently for 10–15 minutes, until the fish is just cooked. Serve hot with steamed rice.

For broiled spiced mackerel, arrange 8 mackerel fillets on a lightly greased broiler rack, skin side up. Make 3–4 diagonal slashes in each fillet. Mix together 2 tablespoons medium curry powder (see page 16), ¼ cup lemon juice, 2 teaspoons each of crushed garlic and ginger, and 2 tablespoons coconut milk. Season and spread this mixture over the fish. Cook under a medium-hot broiler for 8–10 minutes or until cooked through. Serve immediately.

spicy crab curry

Serves **4**
Preparation time **15 minutes**
Cooking time **40 minutes**

2 **cooked fresh crabs**, about
   1½ lb each
3 **onions**, finely chopped
6 **garlic cloves**, finely chopped
1 tablespoon peeled and finely
   grated **fresh ginger root**
½ teaspoon **fenugreek seeds**
10 **curry leaves**
1 **cinnamon stick**
2 teaspoons **chili powder**
1 teaspoon **ground turmeric**
1¾ cup **coconut milk**
salt and **black pepper**

Divide each crab into portions by first removing the main shell. Next remove the two large claws and use a sharp knife to cut the body into 2 pieces, leaving the legs attached.

Put the onion, garlic, ginger, fenugreek, curry leaves, cinnamon, chile, turmeric, and coconut milk in a large saucepan. Season to taste, cover, and simmer gently for 30 minutes.

Add the crabs to the simmering sauce and cook for 10 minutes to heat through. Serve immediately, with plenty of napkins.

For spicy crab with angel hair pasta, cook 12 oz angel hair pasta according to package directions. Meanwhile, heat 1 tablespoon peanut oil in a large skillet over gentle heat and add 3 finely chopped garlic cloves, 1 finely chopped red chile, 6 finely chopped scallions, ⅓ cup coconut milk, and 13 oz white crabmeat. Season and stir-fry for 3–4 minutes. Drain the pasta and add to the crab mixture. Toss to mix well and serve immediately.

sri lankan scallop curry

Serves **4**
Preparation time **10 minutes**
Cooking time **20–25 minutes**

1 tablespoon **peanut oil**
¼ teaspoon **turmeric**
1 teaspoon **cumin seeds**
2 **fresh red chiles**, seeded
   and chopped
1 **onion**, finely chopped
6 **tomatoes**, peeled, seeded,
   and diced
3 tablespoons **medium curry
   powder** (see page 16)
1 tablespoon **coconut milk**
1 teaspoon **ground cumin**
1 teaspoon **garam masala**
13 oz fresh **scallops**
small handful of finely chopped
   cilantro leaves
salt and **black pepper**

Heat the oil in a skillet over low heat. Add the turmeric, cumin seeds, and chiles, and sauté briefly to release the flavors. Add the onion and cook gently for 10 minutes, until softened but not colored.

Stir in the tomatoes and curry powder and simmer for 5 minutes or until the tomatoes have cooked down to a thick sauce. Stir in the coconut milk, ground cumin, and garam masala and season to taste.

Add the scallops and cook for a few minutes, until the scallops are just cooked through. Check the seasoning and adjust, if necessary. Stir in the cilantro and serve immediately.

For homemade garam masala, place ¼ cup coriander seeds, 2 tablespoons cumin seeds, 1 tablespoon black peppercorns, 1 tablespoon ground ginger, 1 teaspoon cardamom seeds, 4 cloves, 1 cinnamon stick, and 1 crushed dried bay leaf in a skillet. Dry-roast over medium-low heat for a few minutes, until fragrant. Remove from the heat and let cool. Transfer the contents of the pan into a mini blender or clean electric coffee grinder, and grind to a fine powder. Store in an airtight container for up to one month, or in the refrigerator for up to three months.

mango & shrimp curry

Serves **4**
Preparation time **10 minutes**
Cooking time **20–25 minutes**

3 **garlic cloves**, crushed
2 teaspoons peeled and finely
   grated **fresh ginger root**
2 tablespoons **ground**
   coriander
2 teaspoons **ground cumin**
1 teaspoon **chili powder**
1 teaspoon **paprika**
½ teaspoon **ground turmeric**
1 tablespoon **palm sugar** or
   brown sugar
1¾ cups **water**
1 **green mango**, peeled,
   pitted, and thinly sliced
1¾ cups **coconut milk**
1 tablespoon **tamarind paste**
1¼ lb **raw jumbo shrimp**,
   peeled and deveined
small bunch of **fresh cilantro**
salt

Put the garlic, ginger, ground coriander, cumin, chili powder, paprika, turmeric, and sugar in a large wok or skillet. Pour in the measured water and stir to mix well. Bring to a boil, reduce the heat, and cook, covered, for 8–10 minutes.

Add the mango, coconut milk, and tamarind paste and stir to combine. Bring the mixture back to a boil, then add the shrimp. Reduce the heat and simmer gently for 6–8 minutes.

Tear half of the cilantro leaves into the curry and cook for another 2 minutes, until the shrimp have turned pink and are just cooked through. Season to taste and serve immediately with steamed basmati rice, garnished with the remaining cilantro.

For chicken & sweet potato curry, simmer the spices in the measured water as above. Omit the mango and shrimp and add 1 small peeled and diced sweet potato and 1 lb diced skinless chicken breasts with the coconut milk and tamarind paste. Bring to a boil, reduce the heat, and simmer gently for 20 minutes, until the chicken is cooked through. Add the cilantro and serve as above.

meat

beef & potato madras

Serves **4**

Preparation time **15 minutes**, plus marinating

Cooking time **2–3 hours**

$^{1}/_{3}$ cup **fat-free plain yogurt**

$^{1}/_{3}$ cup **Madras curry powder**

1 $^{1}/_{4}$ lb **lean tenderloin steak**, cubed

2 tablespoons **peanut oil**

1 large **onion**, thinly sliced

3 **garlic cloves**, crushed

1 teaspoon peeled and finely grated **fresh ginger root**

2 **red-skinned** or **white round potatoes**, peeled and cut into 1 inch chunks

1 (14 $^{1}/_{2}$ oz) can **diced tomatoes**

1 $^{3}/_{4}$ cups **beef stock**

$^{1}/_{4}$ teaspoon **garam masala**

salt

chopped **cilantro leaves**, to garnish

Mix the yogurt with the curry powder in a large nonmetallic bowl. Add the meat, toss to combine, season to taste, and marinate in the refrigerator for 24 hours.

Heat the oil in a large nonstick wok or skillet with a lid over medium heat. Add the onion and stir-fry for 4–5 minutes, until soft. Add the garlic and ginger, and stir-fry for another 30 seconds.

Reduce the heat to low and add the marinated meat. Stir-fry for 10–15 minutes. Add the potatoes, tomatoes, and stock and bring to a boil. Reduce the heat to very low (using a heat diffuser if possible), cover the pan tightly, and simmer gently for 1 $^{1}/_{2}$–2 hours, stirring occasionally, until the meat is meltingly tender. Check the seasoning and adjust, if necessary. Serve garnished with chopped cilantro.

For homemade Madras curry powder, dry-roast

$^{1}/_{2}$ cup coriander seeds, $^{1}/_{3}$ cup cumin seeds, 1 tablespoon black mustard seeds, and 1 tablespoon fennel seeds in a nonstick skillet over low heat until they begin to "pop." Add $^{1}/_{4}$ cup ground cinnamon, $^{1}/_{2}$ cup black peppercorns, 1 teaspoon grated nutmeg, 1 tablespoon cloves, 2 tablespoons ground cardamom, 2 tablespoons ground turmeric, 2 tablespoons ground ginger, and 2 tablespoons hot chili powder. Continue to heat and stir gently for 2 minutes. Let cool, transfer the contents of the pan into a mini blender or clean electric coffee grinder, and grind to a fine powder. Store in an airtight container for up to one month, or in the refrigerator for up to three months.

pork & lemon grass curry

Serves **4**
Preparation time **20 minutes**
Cooking time **about 1 hour**

1 tablespoon **peanut oil**
6 **shallots**, finely chopped
1 **fresh red chile,** thinly sliced
2 teaspoons peeled and finely
grated **galangal**
1/3 cup finely chopped **lemon grass** (tough outer leaves removed)
2 teaspoons finely grated **garlic**
2 teaspoons crushed **fenugreek seeds**
1 tablespoon **ground cumin**
1 teaspoon **ground turmeric**
1 tablespoon **tamarind paste**
finely grated rind and juice of **1 lime**
3/4 cup **coconut milk**
3/4 cup **chicken stock**
12 baby **new potatoes**
2 **red bell peppers**, cored, seeded, and cubed
1 1/4 lb lean **pork tenderloin**, cubed
salt and **black pepper**

Heat the oil in a large nonstick wok or skillet over medium-high heat. Add the shallots, chile, galangal, lemon grass, garlic, fenugreek seeds, cumin, and turmeric, and stir-fry for 2–3 minutes, until soft and fragrant.

Stir in the tamarind, lime rind and juice, coconut milk, stock, potatoes, and red bell pepper, and bring to a boil. Reduce the heat and simmer, covered, for 25 minutes, stirring occasionally.

Add the pork and season to taste. Simmer gently, uncovered, for 25–30 minutes or until tender. Ladle into warmed bowls and serve with rice.

For curried pork & lemon grass patties, put 1 1/2 lb ground pork in a large bowl with 1 chopped red chile, 4 sliced scallions, the grated rind and juice of 1 lime, 1 tablespoon soy sauce, 2 tablespoons lemon grass paste, and 1/4 cup chopped cilantro leaves. Add enough beaten egg, about 1 extra-large egg, to bring it all together. Shape into 8 patties and arrange on a plate lined with wax paper. Cover and chill for 3–4 hours or overnight. Transfer the patties to a broiler rack, spray with cooking oil spray and cook under a preheated broiler for 6–8 minutes on each side or until cooked through.

pea & lamb korma

Serves **4**
Preparation time **10 minutes**
Cooking time **30 minutes**

2 tablespoons **peanut oil**
1 **onion**, chopped
2 **garlic cloves**, crushed
2 **red-skinned** or **white round
   potatoes**, diced
1 lb **ground lamb**
1 tablespoon **korma curry
   powder**
1 1/3 cups fresh or frozen **peas**
1 cup **vegetable stock**
2 tablespoons **mango
   chutney**
salt and **black pepper**
chopped **cilantro leaves**,
   to garnish

Heat the oil in a large saucepan, add the onion and
garlic, and cook for 5 minutes, until the onion is soft and
starting to brown. Add the potatoes and lamb and cook,
stirring and breaking up the meat with a wooden spoon,
for 5 minutes or until the lamb has browned.

Add the curry powder and cook, stirring, for 1 minute.
Add the remaining ingredients and season to taste.
Bring to a boil, reduce the heat, cover tightly, and
simmer for 20 minutes.

Garnish with cilantro and serve with plain yogurt
and chapatis or pita breads.

For spicy Indian wraps, toss 4 cups finely shredded
iceberg lettuce in a bowl with 1 shredded carrot.
Heat 8 large flour tortillas on a ridged grill pan for
1–2 minutes on each side and then pile some
of the lettuce mixture in the center of each. Divide
the korma mixture (cooked as above) among the wraps
and roll up to enclose the filling. Serve with plain yogurt.

slow-cooked aromatic pork curry

Serves **4**
Preparation time **10 minutes**
Cooking time **2½–3 hours**

1½ lb **pork belly**, trimmed and
    cubed
1¾ cups **chicken stock**
¹⁄₃ cup **light soy sauce**
finely grated rind and juice of
    1 large **orange**
1 tablespoon peeled and finely
    shredded **fresh ginger root**
2 **garlic cloves**, sliced
1 dried **red Kashmiri chile**
2 tablespoons **medium curry**
    powder (see page 18)
1 tablespoon **hot chili powder**
1 tablespoon packed **dark**
    brown sugar
3 **cinnamon sticks**
3 **cloves**
10 **black peppercorns**
2–3 **star anise**
salt

Put the pork in a large saucepan or casserole, cover with water, and bring to a boil over high heat. Cover, reduce the heat, and simmer gently for 30 minutes. Drain and return the pork to the pan with the remaining ingredients. Season to taste.

Add just enough water to cover the pork and bring to a boil over high heat. Cover tightly, reduce the heat to low, and cook gently for 1½ hours, stirring occasionally.

Remove the lid and simmer, uncovered, for 30 minutes, stirring occasionally, until the meat is meltingly tender. Serve with steamed Asian greens and rice.

For slow-cooked aromatic lamb curry, heat 1 tablespoon peanut oil in a large saucepan over high heat. Add 1½ lb lean cubed lamb and brown for 4–5 minutes. Stir in 1 coarsely chopped onion, 4 sliced garlic cloves, 2 teaspoons grated ginger, 2 dried red Kashmiri chiles, 1 cinnamon stick, 1 star anise, 4 green cardamom pods, and 2 tablespoons mild curry powder (see page 16). Stir-fry for 2–3 minutes and then add 4 peeled, seeded, and coarsely chopped tomatoes and 3 cups lamb or chicken stock. Bring to a boil, cover, and gently cook for 1½ hours or until the lamb is meltingly tender. Serve with steamed rice.

fragrant vietnamese beef curry

Serves **4**
Preparation time **15 minutes**
Cooking time **20–25 minutes**

2 tablespoons **peanut oil**
1½ lb thin-cut **tenderloin**
  steak, cut into strips
1 **onion**, finely sliced
4 **garlic cloves**, crushed
1 **fresh red chile,** finely sliced
2 **star anise**
1 teaspoon **cardamom seeds**,
  crushed
1 **cinnamon stick**
3 cups trimmed **green beans**
1 **carrot**, cut into batons
2 tablespoons **Thai fish sauce**
2 tablespoons **ground bean**
  sauce

To garnish
small handful of finely chopped
  cilantro leaves
small handful of finely chopped
  mint leaves

Heat half the oil in a large nonstick skillet and stir-fry the beef, in batches, for 1–2 minutes. Remove with a slotted spoon and keep warm.

Heat the remaining oil in the skillet and stir-fry the onion for 4–5 minutes, until softened, then add the garlic, chile, star anise, cardamom, cinnamon, beans, and carrot. Stir-fry for 6–8 minutes.

Return the beef to the pan with the fish sauce and ground bean sauce. Stir-fry for 3–4 minutes or until heated through. Remove from the heat and sprinkle with the chopped herbs just before serving.

For fresh beef spring rolls, soak 8 large rice paper wrappers in warm water for 3–4 minutes or until soft and pliable. Pat dry with paper towels and spread out on a clean work surface. Thinly shred 6 iceberg lettuce leaves and divide among the wrappers. Top each with 3 tablespoons of the beef curry, cooked as above, arranged in a neat pile along the middles of the wrappers. Turn up the bottom of the wrapper to cover the filling, then carefully turn the two sides in and gently roll up. Transfer to a serving plate and cover with a damp cloth while you make the remaining rolls. Serve immediately or the wrappers will dry out and become tough.

spicy marinated lamb chops

Serves **4**

Preparation time **10 minutes**, plus marinating

Cooking time **8–10 minutes**

12 **lamb chops**

½ cup **fat-free plain yogurt**

¼ cup **tomato paste**

¼ cup **medium curry paste**

1 teaspoon grated **garlic**

1 teaspoon peeled and finely grated **fresh ginger root**

large pinch of **sea salt**

3 tablespoons **lemon juice**

To serve

1 **red onion**, sliced

4 **tomatoes**, sliced

½ **cucumber**, sliced

Arrange the chops in a single layer in a shallow nonmetallic dish. Mix the yogurt with the tomato paste, curry paste, garlic, ginger, sea salt, and lemon juice, and rub into the lamb. Cover and marinate in the refrigerator for 4–5 hours or overnight.

Preheat the oven to 425°F and line a large roasting pan with aluminum foil. Arrange the chops in a single layer in the pan and cook in the preheated oven for 8–10 minutes, turning halfway through cooking, or until the lamb is cooked to your liking. Serve immediately with onion rings and tomato and cucumber slices.

For spicy beef skewers, cut 1 ½ lb lean tenderloin steak into large cubes and place in a nonmetallic dish. Mix together the marinade as above and pour it over the beef. Toss to mix well and marinate in the refrigerator for 6–8 hours or overnight. When ready to cook, thread the marinated beef onto 8 metal skewers and broil under a medium-hot broiler for 3–4 minutes on each side or until cooked to your liking. Serve with warm naans or pita bread and cucumber & mint raita (see page 200).

curried veal pie

Serves **4**
Preparation time **10 minutes**
Cooking time **1 hour**

cooking oil spray
1 lb **ground veal**
1 large **onion**, finely chopped
2 **garlic cloves**, crushed
2 tablespoons **hot curry powder** (see page 16)
3 tablespoons **mango chutney**
1 1/3 cups fresh or frozen **peas**
1 large **carrot**, finely diced
1/3 cup **golden raisins**
1 3/4 cups **fat-free plain yogurt**
4 extra-large **eggs**
large handful of finely chopped **cilantro leaves**
salt and **black pepper**

Preheat the oven to 350°F. Spray a large nonstick skillet with cooking oil spray and place over medium heat. Add the veal and stir-fry for 2–3 minutes, stirring constantly, until the meat changes color. Add the onion and cook for another 4–5 minutes, stirring occasionally, until the onion starts to soften and the veal is lightly browned.

Add the garlic and curry powder and sauté for 1–2 minutes to let the spices cook. Remove the pan from the heat and stir in the mango chutney, peas, carrot, and golden raisins.

Spoon the mixture into a shallow ovenproof dish and press down well with the back of a spoon. Whisk the yogurt with the eggs, stir in the chopped cilantro, and season to taste. Pour the yogurt mixture over the meat to cover evenly. Cook in the preheated oven for 45–50 minutes, until the mixture is piping hot and the top is set and golden. Serve with a crisp green salad.

For spicy veal & pea curry, spray a large saucepan with cooking oil spray and add 1 finely chopped onion. Cook over low heat for 15–20 minutes, until soft. Add 2 teaspoons each of grated garlic and fresh ginger root, 2 finely sliced red chiles, 1 tablespoon cumin seeds, and 2 tablespoons hot curry paste and stir-fry over high heat for 1–2 minutes. Add 1 1/2 lb ground veal and stir-fry for 3–4 minutes, then add 1 (14 1/2 oz) can diced tomatoes, 1 teaspoon agave syrup, and 1/4 cup tomato paste and bring to a boil. Season, cover, and cook gently for 1 1/2 hours. About 10 minutes before the end of cooking, add 2 tablespoons coconut milk and 1 1/3 cups peas. Serve with rice.

goan pork vindaloo

Serves **4**

Preparation time **25 minutes**, plus marinating

Cooking time **1 hour 40 minutes**

2 teaspoons **cumin seeds**, dry-roasted

6 dried **red chiles**

1 teaspoon **cardamom seeds**, crushed

1 **cinnamon stick**

10 **black peppercorns**

8 **garlic cloves**, crushed

¹/₃ cup **wine vinegar**

1¼ lb **boneless pork**, cubed

1 tablespoon **peanut oil**

1 **onion**, finely chopped

2 tablespoons **hot curry powder** (see page 16)

4 **red-skinned** or **white round potatoes**, peeled and quartered

¹/₃ cup **tomato paste**

1 tablespoon **sugar**

1 (14½ oz) can **diced tomatoes**

1 cup **chicken stock**

salt and **black pepper**

Put the cumin, chiles, cardamom, cinnamon, peppercorns, garlic, and vinegar into a mini blender and blend to a smooth paste. Put the pork in a nonmetallic dish and pour the paste over the meat. Rub it into the pork, cover, and marinate in the refrigerator for up to 24 hours.

Heat the oil in a large saucepan and add the onion. Stir-fry for 3–4 minutes, then add the curry powder and pork. Stir-fry for 3–4 minutes, then stir in the potatoes, tomato paste, sugar, diced tomatoes, and stock.

Season and bring to a boil. Cover tightly and reduce the heat to low. Simmer for 1½ hours or until the pork is tender. Serve immediately with steamed white rice.

For papaya and mint raita, to serve as an accompaniment, mix 1 cup fat-free plain yogurt with a handful of chopped mint leaves. Halve, seed, and peel 1 small papaya, then dice the flesh and mix into the minted yogurt.

caribbean lamb stoba

Serves **4**
Preparation time **25 minutes**
Cooking time **1¾ hours**

2 tablespoons **peanut oil**
1½ lb **lean lamb**, cubed
2 **onions**, finely chopped
2 teaspoons finely grated
  fresh ginger root
1 **scotch bonnet chile**, thinly
  sliced
1 **red bell pepper,** cored,
  seeded, and coarsely
  chopped
2 teaspoons **ground allspice**
3 teaspoons **ground cumin**
1 **cinnamon stick**
pinch of grated **nutmeg**
1 (14½ oz) can **diced**
  tomatoes
18 **cherry tomatoes**
finely grated rind and juice of
  2 **limes**
¼ cup firmly packed **brown**
  sugar
1⅓ cups fresh or frozen **peas**
salt and **black pepper**

Heat half the oil in a large saucepan. Brown the lamb, in batches, for 3–4 minutes. Remove with a slotted spoon and set aside.

Heat the remaining oil in the saucepan and add the onion, ginger, chile, red bell pepper, and spices. Stir-fry for 3–4 minutes, then add the lamb with the canned and cherry tomatoes, lime rind and juice, and sugar. Season and bring to a boil. Reduce the heat, cover tightly, and simmer gently for 1½ hours or until the lamb is tender.

Stir in the peas 5 minutes before serving on warmed plates with rice.

For Caribbean lamb, sweet potato & okra stoba, add 3 cups peeled and cubed sweet potatoes after 30 minutes of cooking. Cook 1 cup trimmed and thickly sliced okra over medium-high heat for about 5 minutes, or until lightly browned but still tender. Add the okra with the peas and finish as above.

liver curry

Serves **4**
Preparation time **10 minutes**
Cooking time **about**
 40 minutes

1 lb **calf liver,** thinly sliced
10 **black peppercorns**
1 tablespoon **peanut oil**
1 fresh **red chile,** finely
 chopped
1 **onion**, finely chopped
3 **garlic cloves**, finely chopped
1 teaspoon peeled and finely
 chopped **fresh ginger root**
1 tablespoon **hot curry**
 powder (see page 16)
1/3 cup finely chopped **lemon**
 grass (tough outer leaves
 removed)
1/4 teaspoon **ground cloves**
1 teaspoon **ground cinnamon**
10 **curry leaves**
1 tablespoon **white wine**
 vinegar
2 cups **coconut milk**
2 tablespoons chopped **mint**
 leaves
2 tablespoons chopped
 cilantro leaves
salt

Put the liver in a small saucepan and add enough water to cover. Add the peppercorns, season with salt, and poach over low heat for about 10 minutes, until the liver is just firm but still pink inside. Don't overcook it, or it will be tough. Remove from the heat and drain. When cool enough to handle, cut the liver into small dice.

Meanwhile, heat the oil in a large skillet over low heat. Add the chile, onion, garlic, and ginger, and sauté gently for 10–12 minutes, until soft.

Add the remaining ingredients, including the diced liver, and simmer gently, uncovered, over low heat for 20 minutes or until the sauce is thick. Serve immediately with naan or pita bread and a salad.

For curried pan-fried liver, season 4 thick slices of calf liver (about 7 oz each). Mix 2 tablespoons medium curry powder (see page 16) with 1/4 cup all-purpose flour and use to coat the liver. Heat a large nonstick skillet over medium-high heat. Spray the liver with cooking oil spray, add to the hot pan and cook for 4–5 minutes on each side or until browned. Remove from the heat and serve immediately with a crisp green salad and crusty bread.

lamb rogan josh

Serves **4**
Preparation time **20 minutes**,
   plus marinating
Cooking time **2 hours**

2 lb **lean lamb**, cubed
1 (14½ oz) can **diced
   tomatoes**
1¼ cups **water**
1 teaspoon **sugar**
2 tablespoons chopped
   cilantro leaves, plus extra
   to garnish

Marinade
1 **onion**, coarsely chopped
4 **garlic cloves**, coarsely
   chopped
2 teaspoons grated **fresh
   ginger root**
1 large **fresh red chile,**
   chopped
2 teaspoons **ground coriander**
large pinch of **salt**
1 teaspoon **ground cumin**
1 teaspoon **ground turmeric**
½ teaspoon **ground
   cinnamon**
½ teaspoon **ground white
   pepper**
2 tablespoons **red wine
   vinegar**

Place all the marinade ingredients in a food processor
and blend to a smooth paste. Put the lamb and
marinade in a nonmetallic bowl and stir to coat evenly.
Cover and marinate in the refrigerator overnight.

Put the meat and marinade in a saucepan with the
tomatoes, measured water, and sugar. Bring to a boil,
reduce the heat, cover, and simmer gently for 1½ hours.

Stir in the cilantro and cook, uncovered, for another
25–30 minutes, until the sauce is thick. Garnish with
cilantro and serve with rice.

For perfect rice, to serve as an accompaniment,
put 1½ cups basmati rice in a large saucepan with
6⅓ cups cold water and a large pinch of salt. Bring to
a boil, reduce the heat, and simmer for 10–12 minutes
or according to the package directions. Drain the rice
in a strainer, then put the strainer over the saucepan.
Cover the whole strainer and pan with a clean dish
towel and let stand for 5 minutes. Fluff up the grains
with a fork and serve.

beef, red pepper & squash curry

Serves **4**
Preparation time **15 minutes**
Cooking time **about 1¼ hours**

cooking oil spray
2 **onions**, finely chopped
1½ lb **lean tenderloin steak**,
  cubed
2 **garlic cloves**, crushed
1 teaspoon peeled and grated
  fresh ginger root
1 dried **red Kashmiri chile**
½ **butternut squash**, peeled,
  seeded, and cubed
2 **red bell peppers**, cored,
  seeded, and cubed
¼ cup **medium curry powder**
  (see page 16)
4 cups **water**
salt and **black pepper**
chopped **cilantro leaves**,
  to garnish

Spray a large saucepan or casserole with cooking oil spray and place over medium-high heat. Add the onion and cook gently for 12–15 minutes.

Add the meat, garlic, ginger, chile, butternut squash, bell peppers, and curry powder, and stir-fry slowly for a few minutes. Pour in the measured water and stir well.

Bring to a boil, cover tightly, and reduce the heat to low. Simmer gently for 50–60 minutes, until the meat and squash are tender. Season to taste, stir in the cilantro, and serve hot with rice.

For lamb, potato & pumpkin curry, substitute 1½ lb cubed lean lamb for the beef and 4 cups peeled and cubed pumpkin for the butternut squash, if desired. Replace the bell peppers with 3 red-skinned or white round potatoes, peeled and cubed, and cook as above. Serve with warmed parathas or pita bread.

bangkok sour pork curry

Serves **4**
Preparation time **20 minutes**
Cooking time **2¼ hours**

1 tablespoon **peanut oil**
1 **onion**, finely chopped
1 teaspoon peeled and finely
  grated **galangal**
3 tablespoons **Thai red curry
  paste** (see page 17)
1½ lb thick **pork cutlets**,
  cubed
3 cups **chicken stock**
½ cup finely chopped **fresh
  cilantro root** and **stem**
2 **lemon grass stalks**, bruised
¼ cup **tamarind paste**
1 tablespoon **palm sugar** or
  brown sugar
6 **kaffir lime leaves**
small handful of **Thai basil
  leaves**, to garnish

Preheat the oven to 300°F. Heat the oil in a large casserole and sauté the onion over medium heat for 3–4 minutes. Add the galangal, curry paste, and pork and stir-fry for 4–5 minutes.

Pour in the stock and add the chopped cilantro, lemon grass, tamarind, sugar, and lime leaves. Bring to a boil, cover, and cook in the preheated oven for 2 hours or until the pork is tender.

Garnish with Thai basil and serve the curry with steamed jasmine rice.

For Bangkok sour pork curry with noodles, cook
8 oz thick egg noodles according to package directions. Fresh noodles, available in the chilled section of Asian stores and large supermarkets, have the best texture, but dried noodles are a good substitute. Divide the noodles among 4 warmed bowls and ladle the curry, cooked as above, over the top. Sprinkle with chopped cilantro leaves as well as the Thai basil.

goat & vegetable curry

Serves **4**

Preparation time **10 minutes**, plus marinating

Cooking time **2–2¼ hours**

large pinch of **salt**

1 teaspoon **black pepper**

1 tablespoon **medium curry powder** (see page 16)

1½ lb lean **goat** or **lamb**, cubed

1 tablespoon **peanut oil**

2 **onions**, halved and thickly sliced

3 cups **lamb stock**

2 fresh **Scotch bonnet chiles**

2 **carrots**, chopped

4 **celery sticks**, coarsely sliced

4 **red-skinned** or **white round potatoes**, peeled and cubed

⅓ cup **coconut milk**

chopped **cilantro leaves**, to garnish

Sift together the salt, black pepper, and curry powder, and rub into the cubes of meat. Set aside for 1 hour.

Heat the oil in a large saucepan over medium-low heat. Add the meat and onion and cook, stirring, for 10–12 minutes, until the meat is browned and well sealed.

Add the stock and chiles, reduce the heat to low, cover the pan, and simmer for 1½ hours or until the meat is tender. Add the carrots, celery, potatoes, and coconut milk, and continue cooking for another 20–30 minutes or until the vegetables are tender and the gravy is thick.

For Caribbean rice & beans, to serve as an accompaniment, spray a saucepan with cooking oil spray. Add 4 sliced scallions, 1 sliced garlic clove, and ¼ finely chopped scotch bonnet chile, and stir-fry over gentle heat for 10–12 minutes, until softened. Add 1½ cups long-grain rice and ½ teaspoon grated ginger, stir well, and add 2 cups vegetable stock, 1 cup coconut milk, 1 (15 oz) can kidney beans, rinsed and drained, and 3 tablespoons thyme leaves. Bring to a boil and season to taste. Reduce the heat to low, cover the pan, and cook gently for 10–12 minutes or until all the liquid has been absorbed. Remove from the heat and let stand, covered and undisturbed, for 10–15 minutes. Fluff up the grains with a fork and serve.

slow-cooked beef curry

Serves **4–6**
Preparation time **20 minutes**
Cooking time **2¼ hours**

1 tablespoon **peanut oil**
1 large **onion**, chopped
1½ lb **boneless beef chuck**
   or **beef round**, cubed
2 tablespoons **tomato paste**
3 **tomatoes**, chopped
1 cup **water**
3 tablespoons **fat-free plain**
   yogurt, plus extra to serve
1 teaspoon **nigella seeds**
salt and **black pepper**

Curry paste
2 teaspoons **cumin seeds**
1 teaspoon **coriander seeds**
½ teaspoon **fennel seeds**
2 **garlic cloves**, chopped
1 tablespoon peeled and
   grated **fresh ginger root**
1–2 small **fresh green chiles**
1 teaspoon **paprika**
1 teaspoon **ground turmeric**
2 tablespoons **tomato paste**
2 tablespoons **peanut oil**
½ cup **cilantro leaves**, plus
   extra to garnish

Put the whole spices for the curry paste in a small skillet and dry-fry over medium heat for 2–3 minutes, until fragrant. Transfer the contents of the pan to a mini blender and grind to a fine powder. Add the remaining curry paste ingredients and blend to a smooth paste.

Heat the oil in a large saucepan over medium heat, add the onion, and cook for 5–6 minutes or until beginning to brown, stirring occasionally. Add 3 tablespoons of the prepared curry paste and stir-fry for 1–2 minutes.

Stir in the beef and cook for 4–5 minutes or until the meat is browned and well coated. Stir in the tomato paste, tomatoes, measured water, and yogurt, and bring to a boil. Reduce the heat, cover, and simmer for 2 hours or until tender, adding more liquid, if necessary.

Season to taste and ladle into warmed bowls. Sprinkle with the nigella seeds and garnish with cilantro leaves. Serve hot with naan or pita bread and yogurt.

For slow-cooked lamb curry with spinach & chickpeas, make the curry as above, replacing the curry paste with ¼ cup store-made Madras or rogan josh curry paste and the beef with 1½ lb cubed lean leg of lamb. Stir 1 (15 oz) can chickpeas, rinsed and drained, into the curry with the yogurt. Cook as above, stirring in 4 cups baby spinach at the end of the cooking time.

stuffed eggplants with lamb

Serves **4**
Preparation time **20 minutes**
Cooking time **45 minutes**

2 large **eggplants**
1 tablespoon **peanut oil**
1 **onion**, thinly sliced
1 teaspoon peeled and finely
  grated **fresh ginger root**
1 teaspoon **hot chili powder**
1 tablespoon **medium curry
  paste**
2 **garlic cloves**, crushed
¼ teaspoon **ground turmeric**
1 teaspoon **ground coriander**
2 teaspoons **dried mint**
1 **ripe tomato**, finely chopped
1 lb **lean ground lamb**
½ cup drained and finely
  diced **roasted red peppers**
  from a jar
2 tablespoons chopped
  cilantro leaves
2 tablespoons chopped **mint
  leaves**
salt

Preheat the oven to 350°F. Cut the eggplants in half lengthwise, use a spoon to scoop out most of the flesh, and discard it. Put the eggplants, cut sides up, on a baking sheet and set aside.

Heat the oil in a large skillet over medium heat. Add the onion and stir-fry for 4–5 minutes, until soft. Now add the ginger, chili powder, curry paste, garlic, turmeric, ground coriander, dried mint, and chopped tomato, and stir-fry for 4–5 minutes. Season to taste.

Add the lamb and continue to stir-fry over high heat for 5–6 minutes, until well browned. Stir in the roasted red pepper and herbs and mix well. Spoon the lamb mixture into the prepared eggplant shells and cook in the preheated oven for 20–25 minutes. Serve immediately with a herbed tabbouleh.

For ground lamb & eggplant curry, heat 1 tablespoon peanut oil in a nonstick wok or skillet, add 1 finely chopped onion, 2 crushed garlic cloves, 2 teaspoons grated fresh ginger root, and 2 sliced fresh red chiles, and stir-fry for 3–4 minutes. Cut 1 large eggplant into ¾ inch cubes, add to the pan, and stir-fry for 2–3 minutes. Add 2 tablespoons medium curry powder (see page 16) and 1¼ lb lean ground lamb and stir-fry over high heat for 6–8 minutes, until sealed. Stir in 1 (14½ oz) can diced tomatoes and 1 teaspoon agave syrup and season to taste. Cook over medium heat for 6–8 minutes or until the lamb is tender and cooked through. Remove from the heat, add a handful each of chopped cilantro and mint leaves, and serve with warm bread or rice.

indonesian beef rendang

Serves **4–6**
Preparation time **30 minutes**
Cooking time **4½–5 hours**

2 tablespoons **peanut oil**
1½ lb **boneless beef chuck**
or **beef round**, sliced
3 cups **coconut milk**
1 tablespoon **palm sugar**
4 **kaffir lime leaves**, shredded
3 **star anise**
1 large **cinnamon stick**
½ teaspoon **salt**

Spice paste
large pinch of **salt**
1 teaspoon **ground turmeric**
½ teaspoon **chili powder**
6 **garlic cloves**, chopped
2 inch piece of **fresh ginger root**, peeled and grated
2 inch piece of **galangal**, peeled and grated
1 teaspoon **black peppercorns**, crushed
4 **cardamom pods**
4 fresh **red chiles**, chopped
2 tablespoons chopped **lemon grass** (outer leaves removed)
3 large **onions**, chopped
1 tablespoon **tamarind paste**

Put the spice paste ingredients, up to and including the chiles, in a food processor until coarsely chopped, or pound using a mortar and pestle. Add the lemon grass and onion, and process or pound to a dry paste. Add the tamarind paste and blend to mix.

Heat the oil in a large saucepan over medium-high heat. Working in batches, cook the beef for a few minutes, until browned on all sides. Remove each batch with a slotted spoon and set aside. Add the spice paste to the hot pan and sauté for 2–3 minutes, stirring constantly. Return the beef to the pan with all the remaining ingredients. Pour in 1 cup water, reduce the heat, and bring slowly to a boil, stirring constantly.

Reduce the heat again to as low as possible and simmer gently for 4–4½ hours, stirring occasionally, until the meat is tender and the sauce has reduced and thickened. Increase the heat and, stirring constantly, cook the beef in the thick sauce until it is a rich brown color and nearly all of the sauce has been absorbed. Serve hot.

For egg rendang, omit the beef and sauté 1 coarsely chopped onion and 2 red-skinned or white round potatoes, cut into large dice, for 5 minutes instead. Add the spice paste and remaining ingredients. Simmer for 1 hour, then remove the potatoes and set aside. Continue cooking until the sauce has reduced and thickened. Return the potatoes to the pan with 6 hard-boiled eggs, peeled and halved, and cook for 5 minutes to heat through.

curried oxtail & chickpea stew

Serves **4**

Preparation time **20 minutes**

Cooking time **about 3 hours**

3 lb **oxtail** or **beef shank,** cubed

1 tablespoon **peanut oil**

2 teaspoons **ground allspice**

2 teaspoons **medium curry powder** (see page 18)

6¹⁄₃ cups **beef stock**

4 **carrots,** cut into chunks

2 **onions,** finely chopped

3 **garlic cloves,** finely chopped

2 **thyme** sprigs

1 fresh **Scotch bonnet chile**

1 (14½ oz) can **diced tomatoes**

¼ cup **cornstarch**

1 (15 oz) can **chickpeas,** rinsed and drained

salt and **black pepper**

Bring a large saucepan of water to a boil. Add the oxtail and bring back to a boil. Reduce the heat and simmer for 10–12 minutes. Drain and pat dry with paper towels. Season to taste.

Heat the oil in a large saucepan or casserole and brown the oxtail on all sides for 6–8 minutes. Add the allspice, curry powder, beef stock, carrots, onion, garlic, thyme, chile, tomatoes, and cornstarch. Stir to mix well and bring to a boil. Cover and simmer gently for 2½ hours or until the oxtail is meltingly tender.

Add the chickpeas and cook for another 15 minutes. Serve the stew immediately with mashed potatoes or crusty bread.

For curried lamb shanks with chickpeas, heat 1 tablespoon peanut oil in a wide casserole and brown 4 lamb shanks on all sides for 6–8 minutes. Add 2 teaspoons ground allspice, 2 tablespoons medium curry powder, 3 cups lamb stock, 1 (14½ oz) can diced tomatoes, 1 finely chopped carrot, 1 finely chopped onion, 4 chopped garlic cloves, 1 thyme sprig, and 1 scotch bonnet chile. Season and bring to a boil. Cover and simmer gently for 2½ hours or until the meat is falling off the bone. Serve with rice or bread.

thai jungle curry with beef

Serves **4**
Preparation time **10 minutes**
Cooking time **about
  25 minutes**

1 tablespoon **peanut oil**
2–3 tablespoons **Thai red
  curry paste** (see page 17)
1 teaspoon **ground turmeric**
¼ teaspoon **ground allspice**
1 lb **lean beef**, thinly sliced
1¾ cups **coconut milk**
1 cup **beef stock**
3 tablespoons **Thai fish sauce**
¼ cup firmly packed **palm
  sugar** or **brown sugar**
¼–⅓ cup **tamarind paste**
salt and **black pepper**

To garnish
½ **red bell pepper,** cut into
  thin strips
2 **scallions**, shredded

Heat the oil in a saucepan and stir-fry the curry paste, turmeric, and allspice over medium heat for 3–4 minutes or until fragrant.

Add the beef and stir-fry for 4–5 minutes. Add the coconut milk, stock, fish sauce, sugar, and tamarind. Reduce the heat and simmer for 10–15 minutes or until the beef is tender. Season to taste and add a little stock or water if the sauce is too dry.

Spoon into serving bowls, garnish with strips of red bell pepper and scallion, and serve with rice.

For Thai jungle curry with pork, replace the beef with 1½ lb pork belly, cut into 1 inch pieces. Add to the saucepan after the curry paste is fragrant and cook for 4–5 minutes. Add the coconut milk, 2 cups vegetable stock, 20 whole small shallots, ⅓ cup roasted peanuts, 1 tablespoon shredded ginger, the Thai fish sauce, sugar, and tamarind paste and simmer for 45 minutes–1 hour, or until the pork is tender. Cook this a day ahead so you can discard any fat that rises to the top on cooling. Reheat it when ready to serve, spoon into serving bowls, and garnish with a few slices of red chile.

nonya meatball curry

Serves **4**
Preparation time **25 minutes,**
  plus chilling
Cooking time **30 minutes**

3 teaspoons crushed **garlic**
²/₃ cup finely chopped **shallots**
1 teaspoon grated **galangal** or
  fresh **ginger root**
6 long **red chiles**, plus extra
  for garnish
¹/₃ cup **sunflower oil**
1 (14½ oz) canned **diced
  tomatoes**
1 tablespoon **kecap asin**
  (Indonesian soy sauce) or
  light soy sauce
1¾ cups **coconut milk**
salt and **black pepper**
chopped fresh **cilantro**,
  to garnish

Meatballs
2 **eggs**
2 teaspoons **cornstarch**
2 **garlic cloves**, crushed
2 tablespoons finely chopped
  fresh **cilantro**
2 **red chiles**, finely chopped
1½ lb **ground beef**

Make the meatballs by combining all the ingredients together in a large mixing bowl. Season well and roll tablespoons of the mixture into walnut-size balls. Put in a pan, cover, and chill for 3–4 hours or overnight if time permits.

Put the garlic, shallots, galangal or ginger, chiles, and half the oil in a small food processor and blend to a paste.

Heat the remaining oil in a large nonstick wok, add the paste, and stir-fry for 1–2 minutes. Add the tomatoes, kecap asin or soy sauce, and coconut milk and bring to a boil. Reduce the heat to low and simmer gently for 10 minutes.

Add the meatballs to the curry and simmer for 12–15 minutes, stirring occasionally. Remove from the heat and serve with rice noodles or steamed rice, as preferred. Garnish with sliced red chiles and chopped cilantro.

For pork meatball curry, replace the ground beef with the same quantity of ground pork, and instead of kecap asin substitute 1 tablespoon dark soy sauce and 1 teaspoon Thai fish sauce. Cook as above.

poultry
& eggs

balti chicken

Serves **4**
Preparation time **15 minutes**
Cooking time **20–25 minutes**

1 tablespoon **peanut oil**
2 **onions**, thinly sliced
2 **fresh red chiles**, seeded
   and thinly sliced
6–8 **curry leaves**
1 cup **water**
3 **garlic cloves**, crushed
1 teaspoon peeled and finely
   grated **fresh ginger root**
1 tablespoon **ground
   coriander**
2 tablespoons **Madras curry
   powder**
1 lb **ground chicken**
2 1/3 cups fresh or frozen **peas**
1/4 cup **lemon juice**
small handful of chopped
   mint leaves
small handful of chopped
   cilantro leaves
salt

Heat the oil in a large wok or skillet over medium heat. Add the onion, chile, and curry leaves, and stir-fry for 4–5 minutes. Add 1/4 cup of the measured water and continue to stir-fry for another 2–3 minutes.

Add the garlic, ginger, ground coriander, curry powder, and chicken, and stir-fry over high heat for 10 minutes. Add the remaining measured water and the peas, and continue to cook for 6–8 minutes, until the chicken is cooked through.

Remove from the heat and stir in the lemon juice and herbs. Season to taste and serve immediately with warmed chapatis or pita bread and plain yogurt.

For creamy chicken & vegetable curry, heat 1 tablespoon peanut oil in a large wok or skillet. Add 1 chopped onion, 1 sliced red chile, 6 curry leaves, 2 teaspoons each of crushed fresh ginger root and garlic, and 2 tablespoons mild curry powder (see page 16). Stir-fry for 1–2 minutes, then add 1 1/4 lb diced skinless chicken breasts. Stir-fry for 3–4 minutes, then add 2 cups chicken stock and 1 cup coconut milk. Bring to a boil and cook for 12–15 minutes or until the chicken is cooked through. Stir in 1 1/3 cups frozen peas and cook over high heat for 4–5 minutes. Season and serve with rice.

chicken kofta curry

Serves **4**
Preparation time **15 minutes**
Cooking time **25 minutes**

1 ½ lb **ground chicken**
2 teaspoons peeled and finely
  grated **fresh ginger root**
2 **garlic cloves**, crushed
2 teaspoons **fennel seeds**,
  crushed
1 teaspoon **ground cinnamon**
1 teaspoon **chili powder**
cooking oil spray
2 cups **tomato puree with
  onions and garlic** or **tomato
  sauce with onions and garlic**
1 teaspoon **ground turmeric**
2 tablespoons **medium curry
  powder** (see page 16)
1 teaspoon **agave syrup**
salt and **black kpepper**

To serve
½ cup **fat-free plain yogurt,**
  whisked
pinch of **chili powder**
chopped **mint leaves**

Put the chicken in a bowl with the ginger, garlic, fennel seeds, cinnamon, and chili powder. Season to taste and mix thoroughly with your hands until well combined. Form the mixture into walnut-size balls.

Spray a large nonstick skillet with cooking oil spray and place over medium heat. Add the chicken balls and stir-fry for 4–5 minutes or until lightly browned. Transfer to a plate and keep warm.

Pour the tomato puree into the skillet and add the turmeric, curry powder, and agave syrup. Bring to a boil, then reduce the heat to a simmer, season to taste, and carefully put the chicken balls in the sauce. Cover and cook gently for 15–20 minutes, turning the balls occasionally, until they are cooked through.

Serve immediately, drizzled with the yogurt and sprinkled with chili powder and mint leaves.

For quick chunky chicken Madras, replace the ground chicken with cubed, skinless chicken breasts and the medium curry powder with Madras curry powder (see page 84). Cook as above and add 2 cups peas for the last 5 minutes of cooking. Serve hot.

tandoori chicken skewers

Serves **4**

Preparation time **10 minutes**, plus marinating

Cooking time **about 10 minutes**

1 cup **fat-free plain yogurt**

3 tablespoons **tandoori powder**

1 tablespoon finely grated **garlic**

1 tablespoon peeled and finely grated **fresh ginger root**

juice of 2 **limes**

2 lb skinless **chicken breasts**, cubed

2 **yellow bell peppers**, cored, seeded, and cubed

2 **red bell peppers**, cored, seeded, and cubed

salt and **black pepper**

Put the yogurt, tandoori powder, garlic, ginger, and lime juice in a large nonmetallic bowl. Mix well, season to taste, and add the chicken. Toss to coat evenly, cover, and marinate in the refrigerator for 6–8 hours or overnight.

Preheat the broiler to medium-hot. Thread the chicken onto 12 metal skewers, alternating with the bell pepper pieces, and broil for 4–5 minutes on each side, until the edges are lightly charred and the chicken is cooked through. Serve with warmed naans or pita breads and chutney or pomegranate raita.

For pomegranate raita, to serve as an accompaniment, place 1 ½ cups fat-free plain yogurt in a bowl. Shred ½ cucumber, squeeze out the excess liquid, and add to the yogurt with a small handful of finely chopped mint leaves, 2 teaspoons lightly dry-roasted cumin seeds, and ½ cup pomegranate seeds. Season, mix well, and chill until ready to serve.

sri lankan tomato & egg curry

Serves **4**
Preparation time **10 minutes**
Cooking time **15–20 minutes**

1 tablespoon **peanut oil**

1 **onion**, finely chopped

10 **curry leaves**

3 **garlic cloves**, finely
chopped

2 teaspoons peeled and finely
grated **fresh ginger root**

2 **fresh green chiles**, finely
chopped

3 tablespoons **medium curry
powder** (see page 16)

1 (14½ oz) can **diced
tomatoes**

8–12 **eggs**, hard-boiled and
peeled

⅓ cup finely chopped **cilantro
leaves**

salt

Heat the oil in a large, nonstick skillet and add the
onion, curry leaves, garlic, ginger, and chiles. Stir-fry
over medium heat for 6–8 minutes.

Sprinkle with the curry powder and stir-fry for another
1–2 minutes, until fragrant. Stir in the diced tomatoes,
season to taste, and stir to mix well.

Add the eggs and bring to a boil. Reduce the heat
and simmer gently for 4–5 minutes. Remove from the
heat and stir in the cilantro. Halve the eggs and serve
immediately with rice.

For Sri Lankan coconut relish, to serve as an
accompaniment, mix 1 tablespoon grated red onion
with 1 crushed garlic clove, ⅔ cup grated fresh
coconut, 1 teaspoon chili powder, 1 teaspoon paprika,
1 tablespoon anchovy sauce, and the juice of 2 limes.
Let stand at room temperature for 30 minutes before
serving with the curry and rice.

bhoona chicken curry

Serves **4**

Preparation time **10 minutes**, plus marinating

Cooking time **8–10 minutes**

½ cup **fat-free plain yogurt**

juice of 2 **limes**

2 **garlic cloves**, finely chopped

1 teaspoon **ground turmeric**

1 tablespoon **mild chili powder**

1 teaspoon **cardamom seeds**, crushed

large pinch of **sea salt**

1 tablespoon **ground coriander**

1 tablespoon **ground cumin**

4 skinless **chicken breasts**, cut into strips

1 tablespoon **peanut oil**

1 teaspoon **garam masala**

handful of coarsely chopped **cilantro leaves**

Put the yogurt, lime juice, garlic, turmeric, chili powder, cardamom, salt, ground coriander, and cumin in a large nonmetallic bowl. Mix well and add the chicken. Toss to coat evenly, cover, and marinate in the refrigerator for 6–8 hours or overnight.

Heat the oil in a large, nonstick skillet over medium-high heat, and stir-fry the chicken mixture for 8–10 minutes, until tender and cooked through.

Sprinkle with the garam masala and chopped cilantro, stir well, and serve with steamed rice.

For masala chicken kebabs, prepare the marinade as above and add 4 skinless chicken breasts, cut into cubes. Marinate in the refrigerator for 6–8 hours or overnight if time permits. When ready to cook, thread the chicken pieces onto 8 metal skewers and cook under a medium-hot broiler for 5–6 minutes on each side or until cooked through. Serve with warmed naan or pita breads or rice.

souffléd curried omelet

Serves **4**
Preparation time **25 minutes**
Cooking time **about
20 minutes**

1 tablespoon **peanut oil**
4 **garlic cloves**, crushed
8 **scallions**, finely sliced
1 **red chile,** finely sliced
1 tablespoon **medium curry
powder** (see page 16)
4 **tomatoes**, peeled, seeded,
and finely chopped
small handful of finely chopped
cilantro leaves
small handful of finely chopped
mint leaves,
8 extra-large **eggs**, separated
salt and **black pepper**

Heat half the oil in an ovenproof skillet over medium heat. Add the garlic, scallions, and red chile and stir-fry for 1–2 minutes. Stir in the curry powder, tomatoes, and chopped herbs and stir-fry for 20–30 seconds. Remove from the heat, season to taste, and let cool slightly.

Put the egg whites in a large bowl and whisk until soft peaks form. Gently beat the egg yolks in a separate bowl, then fold into the egg whites with the tomato mixture until well combined.

Wipe out the pan with paper towels and place over medium heat. Add the remaining oil and, when hot, pour in the egg mixture. Reduce the heat and cook gently for 8–10 minutes or until the bottom is starting to set. Transfer the pan to a preheated medium-hot broiler and cook for 4–5 minutes or until the top is puffed, lightly golden, and almost set. Serve immediately with toast and a crisp green salad.

For Indian spicy scrambled eggs, heat 1 tablespoon peanut oil in a large nonstick skillet over a gentle heat. Beat 8 eggs in a bowl and add 1 finely chopped red onion, 2 sliced green chiles, 1 finely chopped tomato, 1 teaspoon grated peeled ginger, and a small handful of finely chopped cilantro leaves. Season, pour into the pan, and cook, stirring occasionally, for 5–6 minutes or until lightly scrambled. Serve immediately with toast.

thai jungle curry with duck

Serves **4**
Preparation time **20 minutes**
Cooking time **30 minutes**

2 tablespoons **Thai green
  curry paste** (see page 17)
2 tablespoons finely chopped
  lemon grass (tough outer
  leaves removed)
3 **kaffir lime leaves**, finely
  shredded
1 teaspoon **shrimp paste**
6 **garlic cloves**, crushed
5 **shallots**, finely chopped
3 tablespoons finely chopped
  cilantro root
2 tablespoons **peanut oil**
cooking oil spray
1¼ lb skinless **duck breast
  fillets**, thinly sliced
1¾ cups **chicken stock**
1 tablespoon **Thai fish sauce**
½ cup rinsed and drained
  canned bamboo shoots
4 baby **eggplants**, quartered
small handful of **Thai basil
  leaves**

Put the green curry paste, lemon grass, lime leaves, shrimp paste, garlic, shallots, cilantro root, and peanut oil in a mini blender and blend to a smooth paste, adding a little water, if necessary.

Spray a large nonstick wok with cooking oil spray, put over high heat, and add the curry paste. Stir-fry for 1–2 minutes, then add the duck. Stir-fry for 4–5 minutes, until sealed, then pour in the stock and fish sauce and bring to a boil. Remove the duck from the pan with a slotted spoon, set aside, and keep warm.

Add the bamboo shoots and eggplants to the pan and cook for 12–15 minutes or until tender.

Return the meat to the pan and cook gently for 3–4 minutes. Stir in half the basil leaves and remove from the heat. Ladle into bowls, garnish with the remaining basil, and serve with jasmine rice.

For jungle curry with pigeon, replace the duck with 8 pigeon breasts, thinly sliced. Follow the recipe above, using light soy sauce instead of Thai fish sauce, and replacing the bamboo shoots with canned water chestnuts for a crunchy texture. Cook as above until the pigeon is tender.

indonesian yellow drumstick curry

Serves **4**
Preparation time **15 minutes**
Cooking time **40–45 minutes**

2 **fresh red chiles,** coarsely
    chopped, plus extra to garnish
2 **shallots,** coarsely chopped
3 **garlic cloves,** chopped
¼ cup finely chopped **lemon
    grass** (tough outer leaves
    removed)
1 tablespoon peeled and finely
    chopped **galangal**
2 teaspoons **ground turmeric**
1 teaspoon **cayenne pepper**
1 teaspoon **ground coriander**
1 teaspoon **ground cumin**
¼ teaspoon **ground cinnamon**
3 tablespoons **Thai fish sauce**
1 tablespoon **palm sugar** or
    brown sugar
4 **kaffir lime leaves,** finely
    shredded
1¾ cups **coconut milk**
juice of ½ **lime**
12 large **chicken drumsticks,**
    skinned
8 oz **new potatoes,** peeled
10–12 **Thai basil leaves,**
    to garnish

Preheat the oven to 375°F. Put the chiles, shallots, garlic, lemon grass, galangal, turmeric, cayenne, coriander, cumin, cinnamon, fish sauce, sugar, lime leaves, coconut milk, and lime juice in a food processor, and blend until fairly smooth.

Arrange the chicken drumsticks in a single layer in an ovenproof casserole and top with the potatoes. Pour the spice paste over the top to coat the chicken and potatoes evenly. Cover and cook in the preheated oven for 40–45 minutes, until the chicken is cooked through and the potatoes are tender. Serve hot, garnished with basil and chopped red chile.

For tandoori drumstick curry, arrange 12 large, skinned chicken drumsticks in a single layer in an ovenproof casserole. Mix 1¼ cups fat-free plain yogurt with ¼ cup tandoori paste and the juice of 2 lemons. Season and pour this mixture over the chicken to coat evenly. Cover and cook in a preheated oven, at 350°F, for 35–40 minutes, then uncover and continue to cook for 10–15 minutes or until cooked through. Serve warm with a crisp green salad.

creamy fragrant chicken curry

Serves **4**
Preparation time **15 minutes**
Cooking time **30–35 minutes**

1 tablespoon **peanut oil**

2 **bay leaves**

1 **cinnamon stick**

1 teaspoon **ground cardamom**

4 **cloves**

2 teaspoons **cumin seeds**

1 large **onion**, finely chopped

2 tablespoons finely grated **garlic**

2 tablespoons peeled and finely grated **fresh ginger root**

1 tablespoon **ground coriander**

1 tablespoon **ground cumin**

¾ cup canned **diced tomatoes**

1½ lb skinless, boneless **chicken thighs**, cubed

1 teaspoon **chili powder**

1 cup **water**

½ cup **fat-free plain yogurt**, whisked

small handful chopped **cilantro leaves**

salt

Heat the oil in a large skillet over high heat. When hot, add the bay leaves, cinnamon, cardamom, cloves, and cumin seeds. Stir-fry for 30 seconds, until fragrant, then add the onion. Stir-fry for 4–5 minutes, until the onion is soft.

Add the garlic, ginger, ground coriander, and cumin, and stir-fry for 1 minute. Add the tomatoes and continue stir-frying for another minute.

Add the chicken, chili powder, and measured water. Season to taste and bring to a boil. Cover the pan, reduce the heat to medium-low, and simmer gently for 25 minutes, turning the chicken pieces now and then. Remove the pan from the heat and stir in the yogurt and cilantro. Serve with steamed white rice.

For quick ground chicken & coconut curry, heat 1 tablespoon peanut oil in a large skillet or wok. Add 1¼ lb ground chicken and 2 tablespoons mild curry paste and stir-fry for 3–4 minutes over high heat until the chicken is sealed and cooked through. Add 1¾ cups coconut milk, stir, and cook over high heat for 3–4 minutes. Season, remove from the heat, and serve with jasmine rice or crusty bread.

chicken, okra & red lentil dhal

Serves **4**
Preparation time **15 minutes**
Cooking time **45 minutes**

2 teaspoons **ground cumin**
1 teaspoon **ground coriander**
½ teaspoon **cayenne pepper**
¼ teaspoon **ground turmeric**
1 lb skinless, boneless
   chicken thighs, cut into
   large pieces
2 tablespoons **peanut oil**
1 **onion**, sliced
2 **garlic cloves**, crushed
¼ cup peeled and finely
   chopped **fresh ginger root**
3 cups **water**
1½ cups **red lentils**, rinsed
8 oz **okra**
small handful of **cilantro**
   leaves, chopped
salt
lime wedges, to garnish

Mix the cumin, coriander, cayenne, and turmeric and toss with the chicken pieces.

Heat the oil in a large saucepan. Cook the chicken pieces, in batches, until deep golden, transferring each batch to a plate. Add the onion to the pan and sauté for 5 minutes, until golden. Stir in the garlic and ginger and cook for another 1 minute.

Return the chicken to the pan and add the measured water. Bring to a boil, reduce the heat, and simmer gently, covered, for 20 minutes, until the chicken is cooked through. Add the lentils and cook for 5 minutes.

Stir in the okra, cilantro, and a little salt and cook for another 5 minutes, until the lentils are tender but not completely pulpy. Serve in shallow bowls with lime wedges, chutney, and poppadums.

For chicken, zucchini & chile dhal, follow the main recipe but replace the okra with 3 zucchini, thinly sliced. For a hotter flavor, add 1 thinly sliced medium-strength red chile with the garlic and ginger.

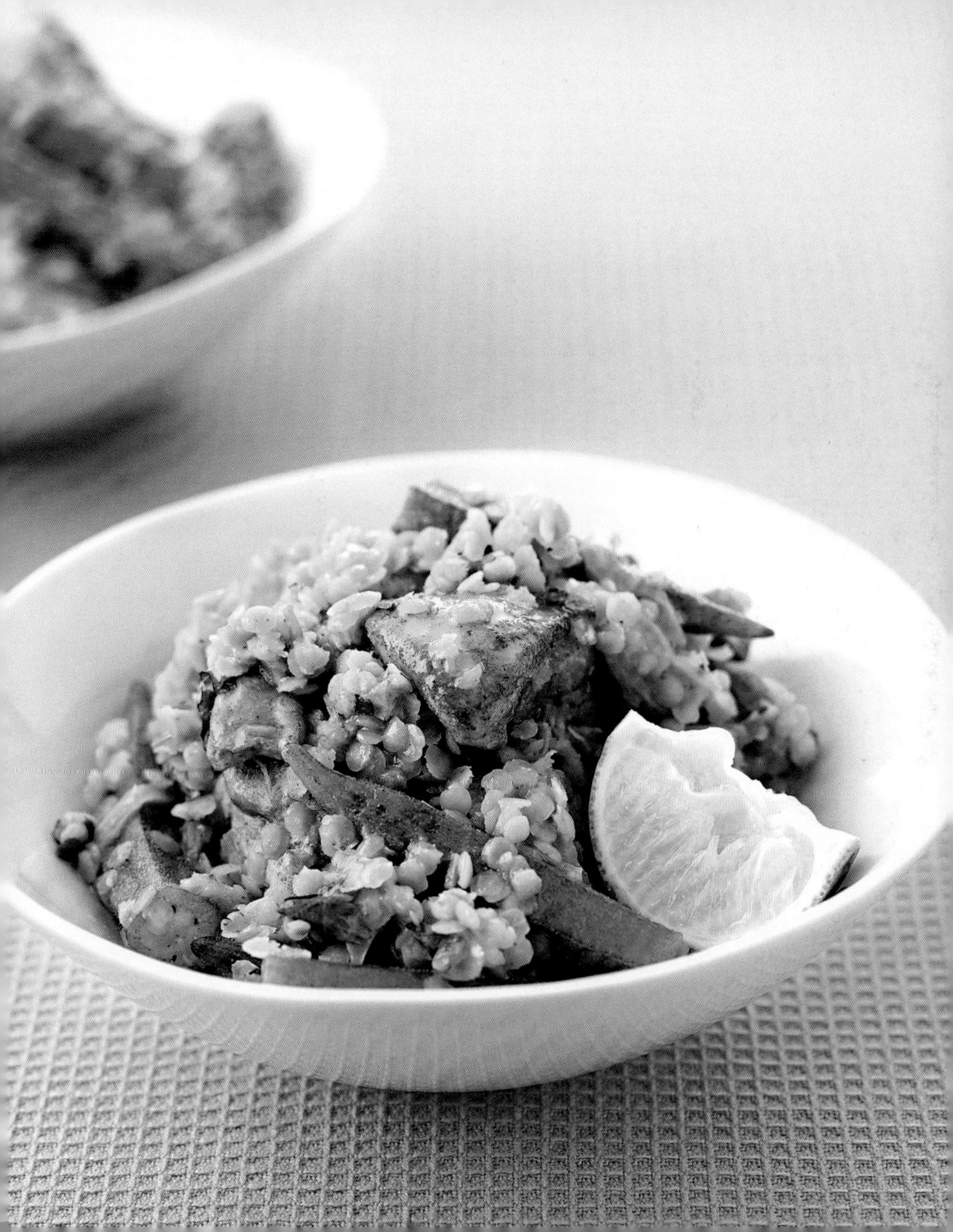

goan xacutti duck

Serves **4**

Preparation time **20 minutes**, plus marinating

Cooking time **40–50 minutes**

1½ lb skinless **duck breast fillets**, cubed

2 tablespoons **dried coconut**

1 tablespoon **peanut oil**

2 large **onions**, finely chopped

1 tablespoon **tomato paste**

4 fresh **red chiles**

1 teaspoon **ground cloves**

2 tablespoons **garam masala**

1 **cinnamon stick**

2 cups **water**

chopped **cilantro leaves**, to garnish

lime wedges, to serve

Xacutti marinade

1 tablespoon **garlic paste**

1 tablespoon **ginger paste**

2 tablespoons finely chopped **cilantro leaves**

1 tablespoon **tamarind paste**

1 teaspoon **ground turmeric**

1 teaspoon **chili powder**

Mix all the marinade ingredients together in a large bowl. Add the duck and toss to coat well. Cover and marinate in the refrigerator for 6–8 hours or overnight.

Heat a small skillet over low heat and dry-roast the coconut for a few minutes, until lightly golden. Remove from the heat and set aside.

Heat the oil in a large saucepan over medium heat and sauté the onion for 8–10 minutes, until soft and lightly browned. Add the roasted coconut, tomato paste, chiles, cloves, garam masala, and cinnamon stick. Stir well to blend. Add the duck with the marinade and stir-fry over high heat for 5 minutes.

Add the measured water and bring to a boil. Reduce the heat to low and simmer, covered, for 25–30 minutes, until the duck is tender and the sauce is thick. Garnish with chopped cilantro and serve with lime wedges for squeezing.

For chicken xacutti skewers, mix all the marinade ingredients in a nonmetallic bowl with 1 cup fat-free plain yogurt. Add 1½ lb skinless, boneless chicken thighs, season to taste, toss to mix well, and marinate in the refrigerator for 6–8 hours. Thread the chicken onto 8 metal skewers and cook under a medium-hot broiler for 5–6 minutes on each side or until cooked through. Serve immediately, garnished with chopped cilantro.

phillipino chicken curry

Serves **4**

Preparation time **10 minutes**,
    plus marinating

Cooking time **40–50 minutes**

1 ½ lb skinless, boneless
    chicken thighs
2 tablespoons **medium curry
    powder** (see page 16)
1 tablespoon **peanut oil**
4 **garlic cloves**, crushed
1 **onion**, sliced
4 small **tomatoes**, chopped
1¾ cups **coconut milk**
1 cup **chicken stock**
3 **red-skinned** or **white
    round potatoes**, peeled
    and quartered
salt

Put the chicken in a nonmetallic bowl and sprinkle with
the curry powder. Toss to mix well and marinate in the
refrigerator for 30 minutes.

Heat the oil in a large saucepan over medium-high
heat. Add the garlic, onion, and tomatoes, and sauté
for 3–4 minutes. Add the marinated chicken and
stir-fry for 4–5 minutes.

Add the coconut milk, stock, and potatoes and season
to taste. Bring to a boil, reduce the heat to medium-low,
and simmer gently for 30–40 minutes, until the chicken
is tender. Serve hot with rice and pickles.

For Phillipino chicken skewers, cut 1 ½ lb skinless,
boneless chicken thighs into bite-size pieces and put
in a bowl with ½ cup coconut milk, ⅓ cup tomato paste,
4 crushed garlic cloves, and 2 tablespoons medium
curry powder (see page 18). Season, toss to mix well,
and marinate for 6–8 hours in the refrigerator. Thread
the chicken onto 8 metal skewers and cook under
a medium-hot broiler for 5–6 minutes on each side
or until cooked through. Serve with lime wedges.

spinach & chicken curry

Serves **4**

Preparation time **15 minutes,**
  plus marinating

Cooking time **about 1 hour**

$^1/_3$ cup **fat-free plain yogurt**

2 tablespoons finely grated
  garlic

2 tablespoons peeled and
  finely grated **fresh ginger
  root**

1 tablespoon **ground
  coriander**

1 tablespoon **medium curry
  powder** (see page 16)

1½ lb skinless **chicken
  breasts**, cubed

3 cups **frozen spinach**

1 tablespoon **peanut oil**

1 **onion**, finely chopped

2 teaspoons **cumin seeds**

1¾ cups **chicken stock**

1 tablespoon **lemon juice**

salt and **black pepper**

Mix the yogurt, garlic, ginger, coriander, and curry
powder in a large nonmetallic bowl. Season to taste
and add the chicken. Toss to mix well, cover, and
marinate in the refrigerator for 8–10 hours.

Put the frozen spinach in a saucepan and cook over
medium heat for 6–8 minutes, until defrosted. Season
to taste and drain thoroughly. Transfer to a food
processor and blend until smooth.

Heat the oil in a large nonstick skillet with a lid over low
heat. Add the onion and sauté gently for 10–12 minutes,
until soft and translucent. Add the cumin seeds and stir-
fry for 1 minute, until fragrant. Increase the heat to high,
and add the chicken mixture. Stir-fry for 6–8 minutes.

Pour in the stock and spinach puree and bring to
a boil. Reduce the heat, cover, and simmer gently for
25–30 minutes, until the chicken is cooked through.
Uncover the pan, season to taste, and cook over high
heat for 3–4 minutes, stirring often. Remove from the
heat and stir in the lemon juice. Serve immediately.

For duck curry with spinach, cut 4 skinless duck
breasts into chunks. Heat 1 tablespoon peanut oil in
a large saucepan over medium-low heat and stir-fry
1 chopped onion for 8–10 minutes, until tender, then add
2 tablespoons each of grated garlic and ginger. Increase
the heat, add the duck and stir-fry for 2–3 minutes. Stir
in 1 tablespoon medium curry powder (see page 18)
and cook for 1 minute. Add 1¾ cups chicken stock and
bring to a boil. Reduce the heat, cover, and simmer for
25–30 minutes. Stir in 5 cups baby spinach and cook
for 3–4 minutes or until just wilted.

chicken mussaman curry

Serves **4**
Preparation time **10 minutes**
Cooking time **35–40 minutes**

1 tablespoon **peanut oil**
1 large **onion**, sliced
¼ cup **mussaman curry paste**
1¾ cup **coconut milk**
1½ lb skinless **chicken breasts**, cubed
2 tablespoons **Thai fish sauce**
2 tablespoons **lime juice**
1 teaspoon **agave syrup**
1 **baby eggplant**, thinly sliced
2 tablespoons chopped **Thai basil leaves**

Heat the oil in a wok or skillet over medium heat. Add the onion and sauté for 6–8 minutes, until soft.

Blend the curry paste with a little of the coconut milk and add to the pan. Sauté for 1 minute, then add the chicken and stir vigorously for 3 minutes. Add the remaining coconut milk, fish sauce, lime juice, and agave syrup. Stir well, reduce the heat to low, and simmer gently for 20 minutes.

Increase the heat to high, add the eggplant, and cook for 6–8 minutes. Remove from the heat, stir in the chopped basil, and serve immediately.

For homemade mussaman curry paste, put ⅔ cup unsalted peanuts in a mini blender with 2 sliced shallots, 2 teaspoons dried red chiles, 2 teaspoons grated galangal or ginger, 2 tablespoons chopped lemon grass, 2 teaspoons each of coriander seeds and cumin seeds, ¼ teaspoon ground nutmeg, 1 teaspoon ground cinnamon, a pinch of ground cloves, 1 teaspoon ground cardamom, 2 tablespoons Thai fish sauce, 1 teaspoon shrimp paste, and 2 teaspoons palm sugar. Add ½–⅔ cup coconut milk and blend until fairly smooth. Store any leftover paste in an airtight jar in the refrigerator for up to one week, or freeze in small portions for later use.

vegetables

potato & green bean curry

Serves **4**
Preparation time **20 minutes**
Cooking time **6–8 minutes**

1 tablespoon **peanut oil**
4 teaspoons **cumin seeds**
1 teaspoon **medium curry powder** (see page 16)
1 **fresh green chile,** finely sliced
2 teaspoons **ground cumin**
2 teaspoons **ground coriander**
1 teaspoon **ground turmeric**
4 **plum tomatoes,** peeled, seeded, and finely diced
1 lb **new potatoes,** halved and boiled
4 cups blanched ½ inch **green bean** pieces
¹/₃ cup chopped **mint leaves**
juice of 1 large **lime**
salt and **black pepper**

Heat the oil in a large nonstick wok or skillet over medium-high heat. Add the cumin seeds, curry powder, and green chile and stir-fry for 1–2 minutes, until fragrant.

Add the ground spices, tomatoes, potatoes, and green beans. Season to taste and stir-fry briskly over high heat for 4–5 minutes. Remove from the heat and stir in the mint. Squeeze the lime juice over the top and serve immediately.

For simple pilaf rice, to serve as an accompaniment, place 1 tablespoon mild curry powder (see page 18) in a medium saucepan with 4 crushed green cardamom pods, 1 cinnamon stick, 2 cloves, and 1½ cups basmati rice. Add 2¾ cups boiling water, season, and bring to a boil. Reduce the heat to low, cover the pan, and cook gently for 10–12 minutes or until all the liquid has been absorbed. Remove from the heat and let stand, covered and undisturbed, for 10–15 minutes. Fluff up the grains with a fork and serve.

curried cabbage & carrot stir-fry

Serves **4**

Preparation time **10 minutes**

Cooking time **about**
   15 minutes

1 tablespoon **peanut oil**

4 **shallots**, finely chopped

2 teaspoons peeled and finely
   grated **fresh ginger root**

2 teaspoons finely grated
   garlic

2 **fresh long green chiles**,
   halved lengthwise

2 teaspoons **cumin seeds**

1 teaspoon **ground turmeric**

1 teaspoon **coriander seeds**,
   crushed

1 large **carrot**, shredded

3 cups finely shredded
 green cabbage

1 tablespoon **curry powder**
   (see page 16)

salt and **black pepper**

Heat the oil in a large, nonstick wok or skillet over low heat. Add the shallots, ginger, garlic, and chiles, and stir-fry for 2–3 minutes, until the shallots have softened. Add the cumin seeds, turmeric, and crushed coriander seeds and stir-fry for 1 minute.

Increase the heat to high and add the carrot and cabbage, tossing well to coat in the spice mixture. Add the curry powder and season to taste. Cover the pan and cook over medium-low heat for 10 minutes, stirring occasionally. Remove from the heat and serve immediately with steamed rice.

For speedy coconut, carrot & cabbage curry,

heat 1 tablespoon peanut oil in a large wok, add 2 tablespoons medium curry paste, 2 chopped garlic cloves, and 1 sliced onion, and stir-fry for 3–4 minutes, until softened. Chop 2 large carrots into ½ inch pieces and add to the onion mixture with 3 cups coarsely chopped cabbage, 1¼ cups vegetable stock, and 1 cup coconut milk. Bring to a boil, reduce the heat to medium, and cook for 12–15 minutes or until the carrot is tender. Remove from the heat and serve garnished with chopped cilantro.

lebanese tomato & zucchini curry

Serves **4**
Preparation time **5 minutes**
Cooking time **40–45 minutes**

1 tablespoon **light olive oil**
1 large **onion**, finely chopped
4 **zucchini**, cut into
  ½ x 1½ inch batons
2 (14½ oz) cans whole **plum**
  tomatoes
2 **garlic cloves**, crushed
½ teaspoon **chili powder**
¼ teaspoon **ground turmeric**
2 teaspoons **dried mint**
salt and **black pepper**
mint leaves, to garnish

Heat the oil in a large saucepan over low heat. Add the onion and sauté for 10–12 minutes, until soft and translucent. Add the zucchini and cook for another 5–6 minutes, stirring occasionally.

Add the tomatoes (including the juices) and garlic, and continue to cook over medium heat for 20 minutes.

Stir in the chili powder, turmeric, and dried mint, and cook for another few minutes to let the flavors mingle. Season to taste and serve with couscous or steamed white rice.

For baked spicy zucchini & tomato, thickly slice 4 large zucchini and arrange in the bottom of a medium ovenproof dish. Mix 1 (14½ oz) can diced tomatoes with ⅓ cup tomato paste, ½ cup vegetable stock, 1 tablespoon hot curry powder, 2 teaspoons each of finely grated garlic and ginger, and 2 teaspoons dried mint. Season to taste and spoon the tomato mixture over the zucchini. Cover with aluminum foil and cook in a preheated oven, at 350°F, for 25–30 minutes. Remove from the oven and serve with steamed rice.

thai squash, tofu & pea curry

Serves **4**
Preparation time **15 minutes**
Cooking time **25 minutes**

1 tablespoon **peanut oil**
1 tablespoon **Thai red curry paste** (see page 17)
½ **butternut squash,** peeled, seeded and cubed
2 cups **vegetable stock**
1¾ cups **coconut milk**
6 **kaffir lime leaves,** bruised, plus extra shredded leaves to garnish
1⅓ cups fresh or frozen **peas**
10 oz **firm tofu,** diced
2 tablespoons **light soy** sauce
juice of 1 **lime**

To garnish
cilantro leaves
finely chopped **fresh red chile**

Heat the oil in a wok or deep skillet, add the curry paste, and stir-fry over low heat for 1 minute. Add the squash, stir-fry briefly, and then add the stock, coconut milk, and lime leaves.

Bring to a boil, then cover, reduce the heat, and simmer gently for 15 minutes, until the squash is tender.

Stir in the peas, tofu, soy sauce, and lime juice and simmer for another 5 minutes, until the peas are cooked. Spoon into serving bowls and garnish with shredded lime leaves, chopped cilantro, and red chile.

For Thai green vegetable curry, use green curry paste (see page 19) instead of red curry paste. Replace the squash with 1 sliced carrot, 1 sliced zucchini, and 1 cored, seeded, and sliced red bell pepper and follow the recipe above.

dry bitter melon curry

Serves **4**

Preparation time **10 minutes**, plus standing

Cooking time **25–30 minutes**

2 **bitter melons**

1 tablespoon **ground turmeric**

1 tablespoon **peanut oil**

1 small **onion**, halved and thinly sliced

1 tablespoon **curry powder** (see page 16)

½ teaspoon **chili powder**

2 teaspoons **agave syrup**

3 **tomatoes**, coarsely chopped

1–2 tablespoons **light soy sauce**

sea salt

Scrape the skin and blisters off the bitter melons with a vegetable peeler, just enough to remove raised parts. Cut the flesh into thin slices. Put the slices in a colander and sprinkle with sea salt. Let stand for 30 minutes, then rinse under cold running water to remove the bitter juices. Drain on paper towels and transfer to a plate. Sprinkle with the turmeric and toss to mix well.

Heat the oil in a large skillet over medium heat. Add the onion and stir-fry for 4–5 minutes. Add the curry and chili powders, agave syrup, and tomatoes and continue to stir and cook for 8–10 minutes.

Stir in the bitter melon slices and cook, stirring, for 10–15 minutes. Season to taste and stir in the soy sauce. Serve immediately with rice.

For dry okra & potato curry, cut 1 lb okra into 1 inch lengths. Heat 1 tablespoon peanut oil in a large skillet over medium heat. Add 1 finely chopped onion and stir-fry for 4–5 minutes, until soft and translucent. Add 2 tablespoons mild curry powder (see page 16), 1 teaspoon agave syrup, and 3 chopped tomatoes, and continue to stir and cook for 8–10 minutes. Stir in the okra and 1 cup boiled potato chunks. Cook over high heat for 6–8 minutes, season, and serve immediately with rice.

spicy goan eggplant curry

Serves **4**
Preparation time **15 minutes**
Cooking time **about
  25 minutes**

1 teaspoon **cumin seeds**
4 teaspoons **coriander seeds**
1 teaspoon **cayenne pepper**
2 **fresh green chiles**, seeded
  and sliced
½ teaspoon **ground turmeric**
4 **garlic cloves**, crushed
1 tablespoon peeled and
  grated **fresh ginger root**
1¼ cups **warm water**
1¾ cups **coconut milk**
1 tablespoon **tamarind paste**
1 large **eggplant**, thinly sliced
  lengthwise
salt and **black pepper**

Dry-roast the cumin and coriander seeds in a nonstick skillet over low heat for 2–3 minutes, until fragrant. Remove from the heat and crush them lightly. Put them in a large saucepan with the cayenne, chiles, turmeric, garlic, ginger, and the measured warm water.

Bring to a boil, reduce the heat, and simmer for 10 minutes, until thickened. Season to taste. Stir in the coconut milk and tamarind paste.

Arrange the eggplant slices in an aluminum foil-lined broiler pan and brush the tops with some of the curry sauce. Cook under a preheated hot broiler, turning once, until golden and tender. Serve the eggplant slices in the curry sauce with naans, chapatis, or pita breads.

For cashew and zucchini curry, add 1¾ cups roasted cashew nuts to the finished curry sauce. To roast, soak in water for 20 minutes, chop, then heat in a dry skillet, shaking regularly, until lightly browned. Replace the eggplant with 4 sliced zucchini and broil as above. Drizzle with walnut oil and season to taste.

spiced potato curry

Serves **4**

Preparation time **20 minutes**

Cooking time **6–8 minutes**

1 tablespoon **peanut oil**

1–2 teaspoons **black mustard seeds**

1 teaspoon **chili powder** or **paprika**

4 teaspoons **cumin seeds**

8–10 **curry leaves**

2 teaspoons **ground cumin**

2 teaspoons **ground coriander**

1 teaspoon **ground turmeric**

4 **red-skinned** or **white round potatoes**, peeled, boiled, and cut into 1 inch cubes

1/3 cup chopped **cilantro leaves**

1/4 cup **lemon juice**

salt and **black pepper**

Heat the oil in a large, nonstick wok or skillet over medium-high heat. Add the mustard seeds, chili powder, cumin seeds, and curry leaves. Stir-fry for 1–2 minutes, until fragrant.

Add the ground spices and potatoes. Season to taste and stir-fry briskly over high heat for 4–5 minutes. Remove from the heat and stir in the cilantro. Squeeze over the lemon juice just before serving.

For quick curried spinach & potato sauté, follow the recipe above, then after the potatoes have been stir-fried for 4–5 minutes, gently fold in 3½ cups baby spinach. Stir-fry for 1–2 minutes, then remove from the heat, squeeze ¼ cup lemon juice over the top, and serve immediately with steamed rice or bread.

okra, pea & tomato curry

Serves **4**

Preparation time **5 minutes**

Cooking time **about 20 minutes**

1 tablespoon **peanut oil**

6–8 **curry leaves**

2 teaspoons **black mustard seeds**

1 **onion**, finely diced

2 teaspoons **ground cumin**

1 teaspoon **ground coriander**

2 teaspoons **curry powder**

1 teaspoon **ground turmeric**

3 **garlic cloves**, finely chopped

1 lb **okra**, cut on the diagonal into 1 inch pieces

1 1/3 cups fresh or frozen **peas**

2 ripe **plum tomatoes**, finely chopped

salt and **black pepper**

3 tablespoons grated **fresh coconut**, to serve

Heat the oil in a large nonstick wok or skillet over medium heat. Add the curry leaves, mustard seeds, and onion. Stir-fry for 3–4 minutes, until fragrant and the onion is starting to soften, then add the cumin, coriander, curry powder, and turmeric. Stir-fry for another 1–2 minutes, until fragrant.

Add the garlic and okra and increase the heat to high. Cook, stirring, for 2–3 minutes, then add the peas and tomatoes. Season to taste, cover, and reduce the heat to low. Cook gently for 10–12 minutes, stirring occasionally, until the okra is just tender. Remove from the heat and sprinkle with the grated coconut just before serving.

For spiced pea & tomato pilaf, place 1 1/2 cups basmati rice in a medium saucepan with 2 teaspoons dry-roasted cumin seeds, 1 tablespoon crushed dry-roasted coriander seeds, 2 teaspoons black mustard seeds, 1 1/3 cups fresh or frozen peas, and 3 peeled, seeded, and finely chopped tomatoes. Add 2 3/4 cups boiling vegetable stock, bring to a boil, and season to taste. Reduce the heat to low, cover the pan, and cook gently for 10–12 minutes or until all the liquid has been absorbed. Remove from the heat and let stand, covered and undisturbed, for 10–15 minutes. Fluff up the grains with a fork and serve.

cauliflower & chickpea curry

Serves **4**
Preparation time **10 minutes**
Cooking time **about**
   20 minutes

1 tablespoon **peanut oil**
8 **scallions,** cut into 2 inch
   lengths
2 teaspoons grated **garlic**
2 teaspoons **ground ginger**
2 tablespoons **medium curry**
   powder (see page 16)
2 cups **cauliflower florets**
1 **red bell pepper**, cored,
   seeded, and diced
1 **yellow bell pepper**, cored,
   seeded, and diced
1 (14½ oz) can **diced**
   tomatoes
1 (15 oz) can **chickpeas**,
   rinsed and drained
salt and **black pepper**

Heat the oil in a large nonstick skillet over medium heat. Add the scallions and stir-fry for 2–3 minutes. Add the garlic, ginger, and curry powder, and stir-fry for 20–30 seconds, until fragrant. Now add the cauliflower and bell peppers and stir-fry for another 2–3 minutes.

Stir in the tomatoes and bring to a boil. Cover, reduce the heat to medium, and simmer for 10 minutes, stirring occasionally. Add the chickpeas, season to taste, and bring back to a boil. Remove from the heat and serve immediately with steamed rice and mint raita.

For broccoli & black-eye pea curry, follow the recipe above, replacing the cauliflower with 3 cups broccoli florets and the chickpeas with 1 (15 oz) can black-eye peas.

vegetable & rice noodle laksa

Serves **4**
Preparation time **20 minutes**
Cooking time **40 minutes**

1 tablespoon **peanut oil**
2 tablespoons finely chopped **garlic**
1 tablespoon peeled and finely chopped **fresh ginger root**
2 **fresh red chiles**, sliced
2 **onions**, finely sliced
¼ cup **laksa curry paste**
1¼ cups **vegetable stock**
8 oz **dried rice noodles**
1¾ cups **coconut milk**
1 tablespoon **chili bean sauce**
1 teaspoon **agave syrup**
½ cup **bean sprouts**

To serve
4 **scallions**, finely sliced
1 **fresh red chile**, seeded and thinly shredded
½ cup finely chopped **cilantro leaves**
3 **eggs**, hard-boiled, peeled, and halved
²/₃ cup roasted skinless **peanuts**, coarsely chopped

Heat a wok or large skillet over high heat. Add the oil and, when it is starting to smoke, reduce the heat and add the garlic, ginger, chiles, and onion. Stir-fry for 5 minutes. Add the curry paste and stock, reduce the heat to low, cover, and simmer for 20 minutes.

Meanwhile, soak the rice noodles in a bowl of warm water for 20 minutes, until tender, or according to package directions. Drain well.

Add the coconut milk to the simmering liquid in the pan. Season with the chili bean sauce and agave syrup, and add the bean sprouts. Continue simmering for another 15 minutes.

Divide the noodles among 4 warmed serving bowls and ladle the coconut broth over the top. Serve immediately with the scallions, chile, cilantro, eggs, and peanuts in individual bowls, from which diners can help themselves.

For spicy vegetable & rice noodle stir-fry, heat 1 tablespoon peanut oil in a large wok over medium heat. Add 1 sliced onion, 3 thinly sliced garlic cloves, 1 teaspoon grated ginger, and 2 sliced red chiles, and stir-fry for 2–3 minutes. Add 1 (1 lb) package of prepared stir-fry vegetables and 10 oz fresh rice noodles. Stir-fry for 3–4 minutes or until piping hot. Stir in 3 tablespoons light soy and 3 tablespoons sweet chili sauce, toss to mix well, and serve immediately.

trivandrum beet curry

Serves **4**
Preparation time **15 minutes**
Cooking time **25–30 minutes**

1 tablespoon **peanut oil**
1 teaspoon **black mustard seeds**
1 **onion**, chopped
2 **garlic cloves**, chopped
2 **fresh red chiles**, seeded and finely chopped
8 **curry leaves**
1 teaspoon **ground turmeric**
1 teaspoon **cumin seeds**
1 **cinnamon stick**
5 **raw beets**, peeled and cut into matchsticks
¾ cup canned **diced tomatoes**
1 cup **water**
½ cup **coconut milk**
juice of 1 **lime**
salt
chopped **cilantro leaves**, to garnish

Heat the oil in a wok or saucepan over medium heat. Add the mustard seeds and as soon as they begin to "pop" (after a few seconds), add the onion, garlic, and chiles. Cook for about 5 minutes, until the onion is soft and translucent.

Add the remaining spices and the beet. Sauté for another 1–2 minutes, then add the tomatoes, measured water, and a pinch of salt. Simmer for 15–20 minutes, stirring occasionally, until the beets are tender.

Stir in the coconut milk and simmer for another 1–2 minutes, until the sauce has thickened. Stir in the lime juice and check the seasoning. Garnish with chopped cilantro and serve immediately.

For spiced beet salad, thickly slice 12 cooked beets and arrange on a wide serving plate with 1 thinly sliced red onion and a large handful of rocket leaves. Make a dressing by whisking 1 cup coconut milk with 1 tablespoon curry powder (see page 16) and ¼ cup each of finely chopped cilantro and mint. Season to taste and drizzle the dressing over the beet salad. Toss to mix well and serve.

mustard, mango & yogurt curry

Serves **4**
Preparation time **20 minutes**
Cooking time **about 20
  minutes**

3¾ cups grated **fresh
  coconut**
3–4 **fresh green chiles**,
  coarsely chopped
1 tablespoon **cumin seeds**
2 cups **water**
3 firm, ripe **mangoes**, peeled,
  pitted, and cubed
1 teaspoon **ground turmeric**
1 teaspoon **chili powder**
1¼ cups **fat-free plain yogurt,**
  lightly whisked
1 tablespoon **peanut oil**
2 teaspoons **black mustard
  seeds**
3–4 hot **dried red chiles**
10–12 **curry leaves**

Put the coconut, green chiles, and cumin seeds in
a food processor with half the measured water and
blend to a fine paste.

Put the mangoes in a heavy saucepan with the
turmeric, chili powder, and the remaining measured
water. Bring to a boil, add the coconut paste, and stir
to mix well. Cover and simmer over medium heat for
10–12 minutes, stirring occasionally, until the mixture
becomes fairly thick.

Add the yogurt and heat gently, stirring, until just
warmed through. Do not let the mixture come to a boil
or it will curdle. Remove from the heat and keep warm.

Heat the oil in a small saucepan over medium-high
heat. Add the mustard seeds and as soon as they begin
to "pop" (after a few seconds), add the dried chiles and
curry leaves. Stir-fry for a few seconds, until the chiles
darken. Stir the spice mixture into the mango curry and
serve immediately.

For spicy mango & mint salad, peel, pit, and cube
4 ripe mangoes. Place in a serving dish with ½ thinly
sliced red onion, 12 halved cherry tomatoes, and a large
handful of mint leaves. Make a dressing by whisking
1 cup fat-free plain yogurt with the juice of 1 lime,
1 teaspoon agave syrup, and 1 finely diced red chile.
Season, drizzle the dressing over the salad, toss to mix
well, and serve.

lime leaf & cashew nut curry

Serves **4**
Preparation time **10 minutes**
Cooking time **50 minutes**

2½ cups **coconut milk**
1 **onion,** chopped
1 teaspoon peeled and finely
    grated **fresh ginger root**
1 teaspoon peeled and finely
    grated **galangal**
2 fresh **green chiles,** seeded
    and finely chopped
10 **kaffir lime leaves**
1 **cinnamon stick**
1 teaspoon **ground turmeric**
2 cups **cashew nuts**
1⅓ cups fresh or frozen **peas**
2 tablespoons chopped
    cilantro leaves, to garnish

Put the coconut milk, onion, ginger, galangal, chile, lime leaves, cinnamon stick, and turmeric in a medium saucepan and bring to a boil. Reduce the heat and simmer for 20 minutes.

Add the cashew nuts and cook for another 20 minutes or until the nuts are tender. Add the peas and cook for 3–4 minutes. Remove the curry from the heat and discard the cinnamon stick and lime leaves. Sprinkle the cilantro over the curry and serve hot with jasmine rice and pickles.

For toasted spicy cashew nuts, place 4 cups whole roasted cashew nuts on an ungreased baking sheet and cook in a preheated oven, at 350°F, for about 10 minutes or until they are warmed through. Meanwhile, mix together 1 tablespoon medium curry powder (see page 16), 1 tablespoon sweet smoked paprika, and 2 teaspoons crushed dried curry leaves and season with sea salt. Toss the warm nuts with the spice mixture until completely coated. Serve warm as a snack or cocktail accompaniment.

laotian mushroom & tofu curry

Serves **4**
Preparation time **15 minutes**
Cooking time **about 1 hour**

1 tablespoon **peanut oil**
6 **shallots**, coarsely chopped
1 **garlic clove**, chopped
1½ inch piece of **fresh ginger root**, peeled and thinly sliced
2 **lemon grass stalks**, cut into 2 inch pieces (tough outer leaves removed)
1 tablespoon **mild curry powder** (see page 16)
1 **red bell pepper**, cored, seeded, and coarsely chopped
2 large **carrots**, sliced on the diagonal
6½ cups thickly sliced large **button mushrooms**,
8 oz **firm tofu**, cubed
4 cups **vegetable stock**
1¾ cups **coconut milk**
salt and **black pepper**
½ cup **bean sprouts**, to garnish

Heat the oil in a large saucepan over medium heat. Add the shallots and cook for 5 minutes, until soft and translucent. Stir in the garlic, ginger, lemon grass, and curry powder. Gently sauté for another 5 minutes, until fragrant.

Add the red bell pepper, carrots, mushrooms, and tofu, and stir well. Pour in the stock and season to taste. Bring to a boil, then stir in the coconut milk. Bring to a boil again, reduce the heat and simmer for 45–50 minutes, until the vegetables are tender.

Ladle the curry into warmed serving bowls, garnish each bowl with a pile of bean sprouts, and serve with steamed rice or bread.

For mushroom & tofu stir-fry, mix 2 tablespoons dark soy sauce with 2 tablespoons oyster sauce, 1 tablespoon lemon grass paste, 1 teaspoon honey, and 2 tablespoons Chinese rice wine or dry sherry and set aside. Heat 1 tablespoon peanut oil in a large nonstick wok. Add 1½ cups drained canned bamboo shoots and 13 oz sliced shiitake mushrooms. Stir-fry for 6–7 minutes or until the mushrooms are softened and lightly browned. Add 8 oz diced firm tofu and the soy sauce mixture. Stir-fry until piping hot and serve immediately.

paneer curry

Serves **4**
Preparation time **20 minutes**
Cooking time **about 30 minutes**

1 tablespoon **peanut oil**
8 **shallots**, finely chopped
2 tablespoons **curry powder**
  (see page 16)
4 ripe **plum tomatoes**,
  coarsely chopped
2 teaspoons finely grated
  garlic
2 **fresh red chiles**, seeded
  and finely sliced
2 tablespoons **tomato paste**
1 teaspoon **palm sugar** or
  brown sugar
²/₃ cup **water**
1 cup **tomato puree** or
  tomato sauce
1 lb **paneer** (Indian cottage
  cheese), cubed
1¹/₃ cups fresh or frozen **peas**
salt and **black pepper**
¹/₃ cup finely chopped **cilantro**
  leaves

Heat the oil in a large nonstick wok over medium-high heat. Add the shallots and stir-fry for 2–3 minutes. Sprinkle with the curry powder and stir-fry for another 1 minute until fragrant.

Add the tomatoes, garlic, chiles, tomato paste, sugar, and measured water, and bring to a boil. Reduce the heat to low and simmer, uncovered, for 15–20 minutes.

Stir in the tomato puree or sauce, paneer, and peas, and simmer gently for 5 minutes or until the paneer is heated through and the peas are cooked. Season to taste, remove from the heat, and stir in the chopped cilantro just before serving.

For spicy paneer bruschetta, finely grate 10 oz paneer into a bowl and add 4 finely diced shallots, ½ peeled, seeded, and finely diced cucumber, 1 finely chopped green chile, a small handful of finely chopped cilantro leaves, 2 tablespoons light olive oil, and the juice of 2 limes. Season to taste and toss to mix. Lightly toast 12 thick slices of ciabatta bread and place on a serving plate. Spoon the paneer mixture onto the toast and serve immediately.

south indian vegetable stew

Serves **4**
Preparation time **15 minutes**
Cooking time **20–25 minutes**

1 tablespoon **peanut oil**
6 **shallots**, halved and thinly
  sliced
2 teaspoons **black mustard
  seeds**
8–10 **curry leaves**
1 **fresh green chile**, thinly
  sliced
2 teaspoons peeled and finely
  grated **fresh ginger root**
1 teaspoon **ground turmeric**
2 teaspoons **ground cumin**
6 **black peppercorns**
2 **carrots**, cut into thick batons
1 **zucchini**, cut into thick
  batons
2 cups trimmed **green beans**
1 **red-skinned** or **white round
  potato**, peeled and cut into
  thin batons
1¾ cups **coconut milk**
1¾ cups **vegetable stock**
2 tablespoons **lemon juice**
salt and **black pepper**

Heat the oil in a large skillet over medium heat. Add the shallots and stir-fry for 4–5 minutes. Add the mustard seeds, curry leaves, chile, ginger, turmeric, cumin, and peppercorns, and stir-fry for another 1–2 minutes, until fragrant.

Add the carrots, zucchini, green beans, and potato to the pan. Pour in the coconut milk and stock and bring to a boil. Reduce the heat to low, cover, and simmer gently for 12–15 minutes, until the vegetables are tender. Season to taste, remove from the heat, and squeeze the lemon juice over the top just before serving.

For spicy tomato, vegetable & coconut curry, follow the recipe above, replacing the turmeric, cumin, and black peppercorns with 2 tablespoons hot curry powder (see page 16), and the vegetable stock with 1¾ cups tomato puree or tomato sauce. Serve with steamed white rice.

tindori & lentil curry

Serves **4**

Preparation time **15 minutes**

Cooking time **35 minutes**

²/₃ cup **green lentils**, rinsed

1 tablespoon **peanut oil**

1 teaspoon **ground turmeric**

2 teaspoons **garam masala**

1 teaspoon **cumin seeds**

1 teaspoon **nigella seeds**

1 **fresh red chile**, finely chopped

1 **fresh green chile**, finely chopped

3 large **tomatoes**, chopped

8 oz **tindori** (ivy gourd) or **bitter gourd**, rinsed and trimmed, or 2 cubed potatoes plus ¼ cup water

2 tablespoons **palm sugar** or **brown sugar**

1 tablespoon **tamarind paste**

²/₃ cup **boiling water**

salt and **black pepper**

Cook the lentils in a saucepan of boiling water for 20 minutes, until soft. Drain well.

Meanwhile, heat the oil in a large saucepan and sauté the turmeric, garam masala, cumin seeds, and nigella seeds for 1–2 minutes or until the spices are sizzling. Add the chopped chiles, tomatoes, lentils, and tindori and bring to a boil. Cover the pan, reduce the heat, and simmer gently for 10 minutes, stirring occasionally.

Mix the sugar and tamarind paste with a boiling water and add to the pan. Stir well and simmer for another 5 minutes. Season to taste and serve with chapatis.

For green mango & red onion salad, to serve as an accompaniment, peel and pit 1 small green mango and finely shred the flesh. Mix with 1 small finely chopped red onion and a handful of cilantro leaves. Cover and chill until required.

watermelon & pumpkin seed curry

Serves **4**
Preparation time **15 minutes**
Cooking time **6–7 minutes**

2 tablespoons **peanut oil**
2 large **garlic cloves**, crushed
2 teaspoons **fennel seeds**
1 teaspoon **nigella seeds**
1 teaspoon **paprika**
1 teaspoon **ground turmeric**
1 small **watermelon**, peeled,
    seeded and cut into ¾ inch
    cubes
juice of **1 lime**
½ cup **pumpkin seeds**,
    toasted
salt
small handful of coarsely
    chopped **mint leaves**,
    to garnish

Heat the oil in a large saucepan over medium heat. Add the garlic, fennel and nigella seeds, paprika, and turmeric, and stir-fry for 1 minute, until fragrant.

Add the watermelon and stir-fry for 4–5 minutes. Remove from the heat, season to taste, and add the lime juice and pumpkin seeds. Toss to mix well and serve immediately with the mint sprinkled over the top.

For minted watermelon, lime & ginger cooler,
put the seeded flesh of 1 small watermelon in a food processor with 1 teaspoon grated ginger, the finely grated rind and juice of 2 limes, ¼ cup agave syrup, and a small handful of finely chopped mint leaves. Blend until smooth and divide among 4 tall glasses filled with crushed ice.

rice, beans & grains

shrimp & cilantro pilaf

Serves **4**
Preparation time **10 minutes**
Cooking time **20–30 minutes**

1 tablespoon **peanut oil**
1 large **onion**, finely chopped
1 fresh **red chile,** seeded and
   finely diced
2 **garlic cloves**, finely chopped
2 tablespoons fresh **curry
   paste** (see below)
1 1/3 cups **basmati rice**
2 1/2 cups **fish stock**
finely grated rind and juice of
   1 large **lime**
1 cup finely chopped **cilantro
   leaves**
10 oz cooked, peeled **shrimp**
salt and **black pepper**

Heat the oil in a large saucepan over medium heat. Add the onion and gently sauté for 4–5 minutes. Add the chile, garlic, and curry paste, and stir-fry for 1–2 minutes, until fragrant, then add the rice and mix well.

Pour in the stock and add the lime rind. Season to taste, cover the pan, and simmer gently for 15–20 minutes, until the stock has been absorbed and the rice is cooked.

Stir in the lime juice, cilantro, and shrimp. Let the shrimp warm through, then serve immediately.

For homemade fresh curry paste, place 2 sliced green chiles in a mini blender with 6 chopped garlic cloves, 1 teaspoon ground cardamom, 2 teaspoons grated ginger, 2 tablespoons grated fresh coconut, 1 teaspoon ground turmeric, 2 cloves, 2 teaspoons cumin seeds, a large handful of finely chopped cilantro leaves, 2 tablespoons malt or white wine vinegar, the juice of 1 lime, and 1/2 cup water. Blend to a smooth paste, adding more water, if necessary. Store any leftover paste in an airtight jar in the refrigerator for up to one week, or freeze in small portions for later use.

chickpea & red pepper curry

Serves **4**

Preparation time **10 minutes**

Cooking time **40–45 minutes**

1 tablespoon **peanut oil**

4 **garlic cloves**, crushed

2 teaspoons peeled and finely grated **fresh ginger root**

1 large **onion**, shredded

1–2 **fresh green chiles**, finely sliced

1 teaspoon **hot chili powder**

1 tablespoon **ground cumin**

1 tablespoon **ground coriander**

3 tablespoons **fat-free plain yogurt**, plus extra to drizzle

¼ cup **tomato paste**

2 teaspoons **garam masala**

2 cups **water**

2 teaspoons **tamarind paste**

2 teaspoons **medium curry powder** (see page 16)

1 **red bell pepper**, cored, seeded, and cubed

2 (15 oz) cans **chickpeas**, rinsed and drained

salt

chopped **cilantro leaves**, to garnish

lemon wedges, to serve

Heat the oil in a large skillet over medium heat. Add the garlic, ginger, onion, and chiles and stir-fry for 6–8 minutes, until the onion is lightly golden. Add the chili powder, cumin, ground coriander, yogurt, tomato paste, and garam masala. Stir-fry for another 1–2 minutes.

Add the measured water and bring to a boil. Add the tamarind paste, curry powder, red bell pepper, and chickpeas and bring back to a boil. Season to taste, reduce the heat to low, and simmer gently for 25–30 minutes, until the sauce is thick and rich.

Divide among 4 small serving bowls, drizzle with extra yogurt, and garnish with chopped cilantro. Serve with lemon wedges on the side.

For chickpea & red pepper pilaf, heat 1 tablespoon peanut oil in a large saucepan over medium heat. Add 1 finely chopped onion and sauté for 5 minutes, until soft. Add 1 finely diced red bell pepper and 1 chopped garlic clove, and continue sautéing for 2 minutes. Stir in 1½ cups basmati rice, 1 (15 oz) can chickpeas, rinsed and drained, and 1 tablespoon medium curry powder, and stir-fry for 1 minute. Add 2¾ cups boiling water, season to taste, and bring to a boil. Reduce the heat to low, cover the pan, and cook gently for 10–12 minutes, or according to the package directions for the rice, until all the liquid has been absorbed. Remove from the heat and let stand, covered and undisturbed, for 10–15 minutes. Fluff up the grains with a fork and serve.

spinach & mung bean dhal

Serves **4**

Preparation time **10 minutes**, plus soaking

Cooking time **about 40 minutes**

1 cup **dried split yellow mung beans** (moong dhal) or **pigeon peas**, rinsed

6 cups **water**

1 teaspoon **asafetida**

1 teaspoon **ground turmeric**

3 cups coarsely chopped **baby spinach**

12–15 **cherry tomatoes**

small handful of finely chopped **cilantro leaves**

1 tablespoon **peanut oil**

2 teaspoons **cumin seeds**

2 teaspoons **black mustard seeds**

2 **fresh green chiles**, seeded and finely sliced

1 tablespoon **ground coriander**

1 tablespoon **ground cumin**

2 tablespoons finely chopped **garlic**

2 tablespoons peeled and finely chopped **fresh ginger root**

salt

Put the mung beans in a bowl and cover with cold water. Let soak for 5–6 hours or overnight. Transfer to a colander and rinse under cold running water. Drain and place in a medium saucepan with the measured water. Add the asafetida and turmeric, and bring to a boil. Boil rapidly for 10 minutes, then reduce the heat to low. Simmer gently for 10–15 minutes, skimming off any scum that rises to the surface and stirring often.

Use a wire whisk to whisk the mixture until fairly smooth. Add the spinach and stir to mix well. Stir in the tomatoes and cook over medium heat for 10–12 minutes, stirring often. Remove from the heat and stir in the chopped cilantro.

Heat the oil in a small skillet over high heat. When hot, add the cumin seeds, mustard seeds, chile, ground coriander, ground cumin, garlic, and ginger. Stir-fry for 30–40 seconds, then transfer the contents of the pan to the dhal. Stir to mix well and season to taste. Serve hot.

For spiced chickpea (besan) flour flatbreads, to serve as an accompaniment, sift 1 cup each of whole wheat flour and chickpea (besan) flour with 1 teaspoon salt into a bowl. Add 2 teaspoons cumin seeds, 1 teaspoon ground turmeric, 3 tablespoons peanut oil, and 2 tablespoons chopped cilantro leaves. Mix well and gradually add about 1 cup water to form a soft dough. Knead on a lightly floured surface for 1–2 minutes, then let rest for 10 minutes. Divide the mixture into 8 and roll out each piece to a 6 inch circle. Brush the tops with a little oil. Heat a nonstick skillet over high heat. When hot, cook the breads, one at a time, for 35–40 seconds on each side, pressing down with a spatula for even cooking.

cauliflower & turkey biryani

Serves **4**
Preparation time **25 minutes**
Cooking time **40 minutes**

10 oz **turkey breast**, cubed
¼ cup **peanut oil**
2 **onions**, thinly sliced
1 small **cauliflower**, cut into
  small florets
2 **bay leaves**
1½ cups **basmati rice**
3 cups **chicken stock**
1 tablespoon **nigella seeds**
salt and **black pepper**
2 tablespoons **slivered**
  almonds, toasted, to garnish

Marinade
1 **onion**, coarsely chopped
2 **garlic cloves**, chopped
¼ cup peeled and coarsely
  chopped **fresh ginger root**
2 teaspoons **ground turmeric**
¼ teaspoon **ground cloves**
½ teaspoon **dried red pepper**
  flakes
¼ teaspoon **ground cinnamon**
2 teaspoons **medium curry**
  paste
1 tablespoon **lemon juice**
2 teaspoons **sugar**

Put all the marinade ingredients into a food processor, blend to a thick paste, and turn into a large bowl. Add the turkey, season to taste, mix well, and set aside.

Heat 3 tablespoons of the oil in a large skillet and sauté half the sliced onion until deep golden and crisp. Remove with a slotted spoon and drain on paper towels.

Add the cauliflower to the skillet and sauté gently for 5 minutes. Add the remaining onion and cook, stirring, for about 5 minutes, until the cauliflower is softened and golden. Drain on paper towels.

Heat the remaining oil in the pan. Add the turkey and marinade and sauté gently for 5 minutes, stirring. Add the bay leaves, rice, and stock and bring to a boil. Reduce the heat and simmer gently, stirring occasionally, for 10–12 minutes, until the rice is tender and the stock has been absorbed, adding a little water if the mixture is dry before the rice is cooked. Stir in the nigella seeds and cauliflower and heat through. Garnish with the crisp onion and toasted almonds and serve immediately.

For cucumber & mint raita, to serve as an accompaniment, put ¾ cup fat-free plain yogurt in a bowl with ¼ cucumber, seeded and grated, 2 tablespoons chopped mint, a pinch of ground cumin, and lemon juice and season to taste. Let stand for 30 minutes before serving.

lamb & red rice pilaf

Serves **3–4**
Preparation time **20 minutes**
Cooking time **1¼ hours**

10 **cardamom pods**
2 teaspoons **cumin seeds**
2 teaspoons **coriander seeds**
2 tablespoons **light olive oil**
1 lb **lean shoulder of lamb**,
   trimmed and diced
2 **red onions**, sliced
¼ cup peeled and grated
   fresh ginger root
2 **garlic cloves**, crushed
½ teaspoon **ground turmeric**
1 cup **red rice**
2½ cups **lamb stock**
   (see below)
¹/₃ cup **pine nuts**
½ cup thinly sliced **dried**
   apricots
2 cups **rocket**
salt and **black pepper**

Preheat the oven to 350°F. Crush the cardamom pods to release the seeds, then coarsely grind the seeds in a mortar and pestle with the cumin and coriander. Discard the pods.

Heat the oil in a small, sturdy roasting pan and sauté the spices for 30 seconds. Add the lamb and onions and toss with the spices. Cook in the preheated oven for 40 minutes, until the lamb and onions are browned.

Return to the stove and stir in the ginger, garlic, turmeric, and rice. Add the stock and bring to a boil. Cover with a lid or aluminum foil and cook over the lowest setting for about 30 minutes, until the rice is tender and the stock has been absorbed.

Stir in the pine nuts and apricots and season to taste. Sprinkle with the rocket and fold in lightly. Pile onto serving plates and serve immediately.

For homemade lamb stock, put 3 cups roasted lamb bones and meat scraps in a large saucepan with 1 large onion, coarsely chopped, 2 large carrots and 2 celery sticks, both coarsely sliced, 1 teaspoon black peppercorns, and several bay leaves and thyme sprigs. Just cover with cold water and bring slowly to a boil. Reduce the heat and simmer for 3 hours, skimming the surface, if necessary. Strain through a strainer and let cool. Store for up to one week in the refrigerator, or freeze for later use.

black lentil curry

Serves **4**

Preparation time **20 minutes**, plus soaking

Cooking time **about 1 hour**

⅔ cup **dried whole black lentils**, rinsed and drained

4¼ cups **water**

1 tablespoon **peanut oil**

1 **onion**, finely chopped

3 **garlic cloves**, crushed

2 teaspoons peeled and finely grated **fresh ginger root**

1 **fresh green chile**, halved lengthways

2 teaspoons **cumin seeds**

1 teaspoon **ground coriander**

1 teaspoon **ground turmeric**

1 teaspoon **paprika**, plus extra for sprinkling

¾ cup rinsed and drained canned **red kidney beans**

large handful of chopped **cilantro leaves**

salt

1 cup **fat-free plain yogurt**, whisked, to serve

Put the lentils in a deep bowl and cover with cold water. Let soak for 10–12 hours. Transfer to a colander and rinse under cold running water. Drain and put in a saucepan with half the measured water. Bring to a boil, reduce the heat to low, and simmer for 35–40 minutes, until tender. Drain and set aside.

Heat the oil in a large saucepan over medium heat. Add the onion, garlic, ginger, chile, cumin seeds, and ground coriander, and stir-fry for 5–6 minutes, until the onion is soft and translucent. Add the turmeric, paprika, kidney beans, and lentils and stir thoroughly.

Add the remaining measured water and bring back to a boil. Reduce the heat to low and simmer gently for 10–15 minutes, stirring often. Remove from the heat and season to taste. Stir in the cilantro and sprinkle with a little extra paprika. Serve immediately with the yogurt.

For whole wheat parathas, to serve as an accompaniment, sift 1¾ cups whole wheat flour and ¾ cup all-purpose flour into a large bowl and add 1 teaspoon ground cardamom and 1 teaspoon salt. Make a well in the center and pour in 1 cup warmed buttermilk and 2 tablespoons peanut oil. Work together to make a soft dough. Knead on a lightly floured surface for 10 minutes and form into a ball. Place in a bowl, cover with a damp cloth, and let rest for 20 minutes. Divide the dough into 12 balls and roll each one out to a 6 inch circle. Heat a nonstick skillet over medium heat. Brush each paratha with a little oil, fold in half, then brush again. Fold in half once more to form a triangle, dust with a little flour, and flatten with a rolling pin to a 6 inch triangle. Cook in the hot pan for 1 minute on each side.

chicken & pickled walnut pilaf

Serves **4**
Preparation time **20 minutes**
Cooking time **35 minutes**

12 oz skinless, boneless
   chicken thighs, chopped
2 teaspoons **Moroccan spice
   mix** (see below)
2 tablespoons **light olive oil**
3 tablespoons **pine nuts**
1 large **onion**, chopped
3 **garlic cloves**, sliced
½ teaspoon **ground turmeric**
1½ cups **mixed long-grain
   and wild rice**
1¼ cups **chicken stock**
3 pieces of **preserved ginger**,
   finely chopped
3 tablespoons chopped
   parsley
2 tablespoons chopped **mint
   leaves**
½ cup sliced **pickled walnuts**
salt and **black pepper**

Toss the chicken with the spice mix and a little salt to coat. Heat the oil in a large skillet and cook the pine nuts until they begin to color. Drain with a slotted spoon. Add the chicken to the pan and sautée gently for 6–8 minutes, stirring until lightly browned.

Add the onion and sauté gently for 5 minutes. Add the garlic and turmeric and sauté for another 1 minute. Add the rice and stock and bring to a boil. Reduce the heat to low and simmer gently for about 15 minutes, until the rice is tender and the stock absorbed. Add a little water if the liquid has been absorbed before the rice is cooked.

Stir in the ginger, parsley, mint, walnuts, and pine nuts. Season to taste and heat through gently for 2 minutes before serving.

For homemade Moroccan spice mix, combine ½ teaspoon each of crushed fennel seeds, cumin seeds, coriander seeds, and mustard seeds with ¼ teaspoon each of ground cloves and cinnamon.

tamarind & red lentil curry

Serves **4**

Preparation time **10 minutes**

Cooking time **about 50 minutes**

1 ⅓ cups **dried red lentils** (masoor dhal), rinsed

1 teaspoon **ground turmeric**

4 ¼ cups **boiling water**

1 tablespoon **peanut oil**

1 teaspoon **black mustard seeds**

1 tablespoon **medium curry powder** (see page 16)

4 **hot dried red chiles**

1 **bay leaf**

⅔ cup **water**

2 teaspoons **tamarind paste**

1 teaspoon **agave syrup**

small handful of chopped **cilantro leaves**

salt

Put the lentils and turmeric in a medium saucepan with the measured boiling water and bring to a boil. Reduce the heat to low and simmer gently for 40 minutes, skimming off any scum that rises to the surface and stirring often. Use a wire whisk to whisk the mixture until fairly smooth.

Heat the oil in a wok or skillet over medium heat. Add the mustard seeds and as soon as they begin to "pop" (after a few seconds), add the curry powder, chiles, and bay leaf. Stir-fry for 5–6 seconds, until the chiles darken in color.

Add the cooked lentils and measured water and season to taste. Stir to mix through. Add the tamarind paste and agave syrup and bring to a boil. Reduce the heat to low and simmer gently for 8–10 minutes. Stir in the cilantro and serve immediately.

For tomato rice, to serve as an accompaniment, heat 1 tablespoon peanut oil in a large saucepan over medium heat and sauté 2 sliced shallots, 2 sliced garlic cloves, and 2 teaspoons cumin seeds for 4–5 minutes, until soft and fragrant. Add 4 peeled, seeded, and finely diced tomatoes and 1 ½ cups basmati rice and stir-fry for 2–3 minutes. Season to taste and add 2¾ cups boiling water. Bring to a boil, reduce the heat to low, cover the pan, and cook gently for 10–12 minutes or until all the liquid has been absorbed. Remove from the heat and let stand, covered and undisturbed, for 10–15 minutes. Fluff up the grains with a fork and serve.

punjabi kidney bean curry

Serves **4**
Preparation time **10 minutes**,
    plus soaking
Cooking time **about 1 hour**

1 cup **dried red kidney beans**
1 tablespoon **peanut oil**
1 **onion**, finely chopped
2 inch **cinnamon stick**
2 **dried bay leaves**
4 **garlic cloves**, crushed
2 teaspoons peeled and finely
    grated **fresh ginger root**
1 teaspoon **ground coriander**
2 teaspoons **ground cumin**
2 tablespoons **medium curry
    powder** (see page 16)
1 (14½ oz) can **diced
    tomatoes**
1 cup **boiling water**
salt and **black pepper**

To serve
1 cup **fat-free plain yogurt**,
    whisked
small handful of chopped
    cilantro leaves

Put the beans in a deep bowl and cover with cold water. Let soak overnight. Place in a large saucepan with double the volume of water and bring to a boil. Boil rapidly for 10 minutes, then reduce the heat to low. Simmer gently for about 40 minutes, until the beans are tender.

Meanwhile, heat the oil in a large saucepan over medium heat. Add the onion, cinnamon, bay leaf, garlic, and ginger and stir-fry for 4–5 minutes. Add the ground coriander, cumin, and curry powder and stir to mix well.

Drain the beans and add to the saucepan with the tomatoes and measured boiling water. Bring to a boil, reduce the heat, and simmer for 10 minutes, stirring often. Remove from the heat and season to taste. Swirl in the whisked yogurt and cilantro just before serving.

For homemade naans, to serve as an accompaniment, sift 3¾ cups whole wheat flour, 2 teaspoons sugar, 1 teaspoon salt, and 4½ teaspoons baking powder into a large bowl. Add 3 tablespoons peanut oil and rub into the flour. Gradually add 1 cup warm skim milk, and mix to a soft dough. Knead on a lightly floured work surface for 6–8 minutes, until smooth. Put back in the bowl, cover, and rest for 20–25 minutes. Divide the mixture into 8 balls and roll each one out into a thick patty. Cover and set aside for 10–15 minutes. Preheat the broiler to medium-high. Roll each piece into a 9 inch circle, brush the tops with oil, and sprinkle with nigella seeds. Cooking in batches, put the breads on a lightly oiled broiler rack and cook under the broiler for 1–2 minutes on each side until puffed and browned in spots.

spiced rice with lentils

Serves **4**

Preparation time **20 minutes**,
    plus standing

Cooking time **20—25 minutes**

²/₃ cup **red split lentils**

1¼ cups **basmati rice**

3 tablespoons **sunflower oil**

1 **onion**, finely chopped

1 teaspoon **ground turmeric**

1 tablespoon **cumin seeds**

1 **dried red chile**

1 **cinnamon stick**

3 **cloves**

3 **cardamom pods**, lightly
    bruised

2 cups **vegetable stock**

8 **cherry tomatoes**, halved

¹/₃ cup finely chopped **cilantro
    leaves**

salt and **black pepper**

crispy fried onions, to garnish

Wash the lentils and rice several times in cold water. Drain thoroughly.

Heat the oil in a heavy saucepan and add the onion. Stir-fry for 6—8 minutes over medium heat and then add the spices.

Continue to stir-fry for 2—3 minutes, then add the rice and lentils. Stir-fry for another 2—3 minutes, then add the stock, tomatoes, and fresh cilantro. Season well and bring to a boil. Reduce the heat, cover tightly, and simmer for 10 minutes.

Remove the pan from the heat and let stand undisturbed for another 10 minutes. Transfer to a serving dish and garnish with crispy fried onions. Serve immediately with pickles and plain yogurt, if desired.

For spiced rice with yellow split peas, use the same quantity of yellow split peas instead of red lentils—they can be treated in exactly the same way. Proceed as above.

balinese vegetable fried rice

Serves **4**
Preparation time **15 minutes**
Cooking time **10–15 minutes**

1 **zucchini**, cut into thick
  batons
1 **carrot**, cut into matchsticks
2 cups halved **green beans**,
1 tablespoon **peanut oil**, plus
  extra for greasing
6 **scallions**, thinly sliced on
  the diagonal
3 **garlic cloves**, thinly sliced
1 teaspoon **ground coriander**
1 teaspoon **medium curry
  powder** (see page 16)
½ **red bell pepper**, cored,
  seeded, and sliced
½ **yellow bell pepper**, cored,
  seeded, and sliced
2¾ cups cold cooked **long-
  grain rice**
2 tablespoons **light soy sauce**
2 extra-large **eggs**
1 tablespoon finely chopped
  cilantro leaves, plus extra
  to garnish
1 tablespoon **water**
salt and **black pepper**
mint leaves, to garnish

Blanch the zucchini, carrot, and beans in a large saucepan of lightly salted boiling water for 2 minutes. Drain and set aside.

Heat the oil in a large wok or skillet with a lid over medium heat and add the scallions, garlic, ground coriander, and curry powder. Stir-fry for 2–3 minutes, then add the bell peppers and stir-fry for another minute. Add the rice and vegetables and stir-fry for 3–4 minutes, then stir in the soy sauce. Toss to mix well and season to taste. Remove from the heat, cover, and keep warm.

Grease a medium nonstick skillet with oil and place over low heat. Whisk the eggs with the cilantro leaves and measured water. Pour the egg mixture into the pan and swirl around. Cook gently for 1–2 minutes, until the bottom is set, then carefully turn over and cook for another minute. Turn out onto a board and cut into thin strips.

Divide the rice among 4 warmed plates and top with the omelet strips. Serve immediately, garnished with extra cilantro and mint leaves.

For quick vegetable curry fried rice, blanch 1 (12 oz) bag of frozen, diced mixed vegetables in a saucepan of lightly salted boiling water for 2 minutes, then drain well. Heat 1 tablespoon peanut oil in a large, nonstick wok and add 2 tablespoons Thai green curry paste (see page 17). Stir-fry for 30 seconds, then add 3½ cups cold cooked basmati rice and the vegetables. Stir-fry over high heat for 4–5 minutes, add ¼ cup coconut milk and heat until piping hot. Season and serve.

dhal makhani with kidney beans

Serves **4**

Preparation time **20 minutes**, plus soaking

Cooking time **about 50 minutes**

²/₃ cup **dried split black lentils**, rinsed and drained

2 cups **boiling water**

1 tablespoon **peanut oil**

1 **onion**, finely chopped

3 **garlic cloves**, crushed

2 teaspoons finely grated **fresh ginger root**

2 **fresh green chiles**, halved lengthways

1 teaspoon **ground turmeric**

1 teaspoon **paprika**, plus extra for sprinkling

1 tablespoon **ground cumin**

1 tablespoon **ground coriander**

¾ cup rinsed and drained canned **red kidney beans**

2 cups **water**

7 cups **baby spinach**

large handful of chopped **cilantro leaves**

salt

1 cup **fat-free plain yogurt**, whisked, to serve

Put the lentils in a deep bowl and cover with cold water. Let soak for 10–12 hours. Transfer to a colander and rinse under cold running water. Drain and place in a medium saucepan with the measured boiling water. Bring to a boil, then reduce the heat to low. Simmer gently for 35–40 minutes, skimming off any scum that rises to the surface and stirring often.

Meanwhile, heat the oil in a large saucepan and add the onion, garlic, ginger, and chiles. Stir-fry for 5–6 minutes and then add the turmeric, paprika, cumin, ground coriander, kidney beans, and lentils.

Add the measured water and bring to a boil. Reduce the heat and stir in the spinach. Cook gently for 10–15 minutes, stirring often. Remove from the heat and season to taste. Stir in the chopped cilantro and drizzle the yogurt over the top. Sprinkle with a little paprika and serve immediately with parathas or pita breads.

For dhal makhani with black beans, follow the recipe above but replace the kidney beans with 1 (15 oz) can black beans, rinsed and drained. Replace the baby spinach with 1½ cups finely shredded green cabbage for a more substantial texture.

tamarind rice

Serves **4**
Preparation time **10 minutes**
Cooking time **about
  20 minutes**

1 tablespoon **sunflower oil**
1 large **red onion**, thinly sliced
2 **eggplants**, cut into cubes
1 **fresh red chile**, seeded and
  thinly sliced
2 tablespoons **tamarind paste**
1 tablespoon packed **dark
  brown sugar**
3½ cups cold cooked
  basmati rice
½ cup **fresh mint leaves**,
  coarsely chopped
7 cups **baby spinach leaves**
salt and **black pepper**

Warm the oil in a large skillet over medium heat. Add the sliced onion and cook for 10 minutes or until lightly browned.

Increase the heat to high. Add the cubed eggplant, half of the sliced chile, a tablespoon of tamarind, and the brown sugar. Stir-fry for 5 minutes, until the eggplant is golden and beginning to soften.

Add the cooked rice, mint, spinach, and the remaining tamarind to the eggplant and onion mixture. Continue to stir-fry for 5–6 minutes or until piping hot.

Sprinkle with the remaining chile slices. Season with salt and black pepper and serve immediately.

For tamarind & dill rice, replace the eggplants with 2 finely diced zucchini and use ½ cup finely chopped fresh dill, instead of the mint. Proceed as above, omitting the chile slices.

chile, lemon & pea pulao

Serves **4**
Preparation time **10 minutes**,
  plus standing
Cooking time **about**
  15 minutes

1 tablespoon **light olive oil**
10 **curry leaves**
2 **dried Kashmiri red chiles**,
  broken into large pieces
2 **cassia bark sticks**
2–3 **cloves**
4–6 green **cardamom pods**,
  crushed
2 teaspoons **cumin seeds**
¼ teaspoon **ground turmeric**
1⅓ cups **basmati rice**, rinsed
  and drained
¼ cup **lemon juice**
2 cups hot **vegetable stock**
1⅓ cups fresh or frozen **peas**
salt and **black pepper**

Heat the oil in a nonstick saucepan over medium heat. Add the curry leaves, chile, cassia bark, cloves, cardamom, cumin seeds, and turmeric. Stir-fry for 20–30 seconds, then add the rice. Stir-fry for 2 minutes, until the grains are well coated.

Add the lemon juice, stock, and peas, season to taste, and bring to a boil. Reduce the heat to low, cover the pan, and cook gently for 10–12 minutes or until all the liquid has been absorbed. Remove from the heat and let stand, covered and undisturbed, for 10–15 minutes. Fluff up the grains with a fork and serve.

For chile, mixed bean & dill rice, follow the recipe above, but replace the peas with 2 cups rinsed and drained canned mixed beans, such as kidney beans, pinto beans, and chickpeas, and replace the chopped cilantro with a large handful of finely chopped dill. Serve with fat-free plain yogurt.

chickpea & spinach curry

Serves **4**

Preparation time **20 minutes**, plus soaking

Cooking time **about 1 hour**

1 cup **dried chickpeas**

1 tablespoon **peanut oil**

2 **onions**, thinly sliced

2 teaspoons **ground coriander**

2 teaspoons **ground cumin**

1 teaspoon **hot chili powder**

½ teaspoon **ground turmeric**

1 tablespoon **medium curry powder** (see page 16)

1 (14½ oz) can **diced tomatoes**

1 teaspoon packed **light brown sugar**

½ cup **water**

2 tablespoons chopped **mint leaves**

3½ cups **baby spinach**

salt

Put the chickpeas in a deep bowl and cover with cold water. Let soak overnight. Transfer to a colander and rinse under cold running water. Drain and place in a wok. Cover with water and bring to a boil, then reduce the heat to low. Simmer gently for 45 minutes, skimming off any scum that rises to the surface and stirring often. Drain and set aside.

Meanwhile, heat the oil in the wok, add the onions, and cook over low heat for 15 minutes, until lightly golden. Add the coriander, cumin, chili powder, turmeric, and curry powder and stir-fry for 1–2 minutes. Add the tomatoes, sugar, and the measured water and bring to a boil. Cover, reduce the heat, and simmer gently for 15 minutes.

Add the chickpeas, season to taste, and cook gently for 8–10 minutes. Stir in the chopped mint. Divide the spinach leaves among 4 shallow bowls and top with the chickpea mixture. Serve immediately with steamed rice or bread.

For curry-filled baked sweet potatoes, scrub 4 small sweet potatoes under cold running water, then prick with a fork. Cook in a preheated oven, at 400°F, for about 1 hour, until tender. Split the sweet potatoes in half and fill with the curry, prepared as above. Top with yogurt and serve.

rice with shiitake mushrooms

Serves **4**

Preparation time **10 minutes**,
  plus soaking and standing

Cooking time **about
  25 minutes**

1 ½ cups **basmati rice**, rinsed
  and drained

2 tablespoons **peanut oil**

13 oz **shiitake mushrooms**,
  sliced

1 **fresh red chile,** seeded and
  finely chopped

1 tablespoon **mild curry
  powder** (see page 16)

1 **cinnamon stick**

2 teaspoons **cumin seeds**

2 **cloves**

4 green **cardamom pods**,
  lightly bruised

8 **black peppercorns**

¼ cup **crisp-fried onions**
  (available from Asian grocery
  stores)

1 ⅓ cups fresh or frozen **peas**

3 cups hot **vegetable stock**

Soak the rice in a bowl of cold water for 20 minutes, then drain thoroughly. Heat the oil in a large saucepan over high heat. Add the mushrooms and stir-fry for 6–8 minutes.

Add the chile, curry powder, spices, and crisp-fried onions. Stir-fry for 2–3 minutes, then add the peas and stir-fry for another 2–3 minutes. Add the rice, and stir for a minute or so to coat the grains.

Add the stock, season to taste, and bring to a boil. Reduce the heat to low, cover the pan, and cook gently for 10–12 minutes or until all the liquid has been absorbed. Remove from the heat and let stand, covered and undisturbed, for 10–15 minutes. Fluff up the grains with a fork and serve with salad.

For quick spicy mushroom fried rice, heat 1 tablespoon peanut oil in a nonstick skillet. Add 8 sliced scallions, 1 sliced red chile, (13 oz) sliced shiitake mushrooms, and 4 sliced garlic cloves and stir-fry for 5–6 minutes. Add 2¾ cups cold cooked long-grain rice, 1 teaspoon sesame oil, and ¼ cup light soy sauce. Stir-fry for 3–4 minutes or until piping hot and serve immediately.

spicy lentil & basmati pilaf

Serves **4**
Preparation time **15 minutes**,
    plus standing
Cooking time **20–25 minutes**

1 tablespoon **peanut oil**
1 **onion**, finely chopped
1 teaspoon **ground turmeric**
1 tablespoon **cumin seeds**
1 **dried red chile**
1 **cinnamon stick**
3 **cloves**
½ teaspoon **cardamom**
    seeds, crushed
1¼ cups **basmati rice**, rinsed
²/₃ cup **dried red lentils**
    (masoor dhal), rinsed
2½ cups **vegetable stock**
¹/₃ cup finely chopped **cilantro**
    leaves
salt

Heat the oil in a large saucepan over medium heat. Add the onion, stir-fry for 6–8 minutes, until soft, then add the spices. Continue to stir-fry for 2–3 minutes, until fragrant. Now add the rice and lentils, and stir-fry for another 2–3 minutes.

Add the stock and cilantro, season to taste, and bring to a boil. Reduce the heat to low, cover the pan, and cook gently for 10–12 minutes or until all the liquid has been absorbed. Remove from the heat and let stand, covered and undisturbed, for 10–15 minutes. Fluff up the grains with a fork and serve.

For tamarind, curry leaf & coconut relish, to serve as an accompaniment, soak 2 teaspoons dried yellow split peas in cold water for 2–3 hours, drain and set aside. Put 2½ cups grated fresh coconut, 2 chopped green chiles, and a large pinch of sea salt in a food processor and blend to a fine paste, adding a little water, if necessary. Transfer to a bowl. Heat 1 tablespoon peanut oil in a small skillet and add 2 teaspoons mustard seeds and the lentils. Cover and cook over gentle heat until you hear the mustard seeds starting to "pop." Add 6 curry leaves and 1 dried red chile and stir-fry for 1 minute. Add the spices and 2 teaspoons tamarind paste to the coconut mixture and stir to mix well. Season to taste.

thai spiced fried rice

Serves **4**

Preparation time **5 minutes**,
  plus soaking

Cooking time **about**
  15 minutes

1¼ cups **jasmine rice**

1 tablespoon **peanut oil**

6 **scallions**, finely chopped

4 teaspoons finely chopped
  lemon grass (tough outer
  leaves removed)

2 **fresh red chiles**, seeded
  and finely chopped

1 tablespoon **Thai green curry
  paste** (see page 17)

2 cups **boiling water**

½ cup **coconut milk**

salt

Thai basil, to garnish

Wash the rice in several changes of cold water, then drain. Soak in a bowl of fresh cold water for 15 minutes, then drain thoroughly.

Heat the oil in a large saucepan over medium heat and add the scallions, lemon grass, chiles, curry paste, and drained rice. Stir-fry for 2–3 minutes, until fragrant and the rice grains are evenly coated.

Add the measured boiling water and the coconut milk. Stir to mix well, season to taste, and bring to a boil. Reduce the heat to low, cover the pan, and cook gently for 10–12 minutes or until all the liquid has been absorbed. Remove from the heat and let stand, covered and undisturbed, for 10–15 minutes. Fluff up the grains with a fork and serve immediately, garnished with Thai basil.

For Thai bean sprout & peanut salad, to serve as an accompaniment, toss 1½ cups bean sprouts in a salad bowl with ½ thinly sliced cucumber, 3 shredded scallions, 1 finely chopped red chile, 1 carrot, cut into matchsticks, and a small handful each of mint and Thai basil leaves. Make a dressing by mixing 1 tablespoon Thai fish sauce with 1 tablespoon lime juice and 1 teaspoon agave syrup. When ready to serve, pour the dressing over the salad, toss to coa,t and sprinkle with ⅓ cup chopped roasted peanuts.

Thai rice with pork & beans

Serves **4**
Preparation time **15 minutes**
Cooking time **15–20 minutes**

1 tablespoon **peanut oil**
2–3 tablespoons **Thai red curry paste** (see page 17)
12 oz **lean pork tenderloin,** finely sliced
2½ cups 1inch **yard long (asparagus) beans** or **green beans** pieces
1 tablespoon packed **palm sugar** or **brown sugar**
5 cups cold cooked **jasmine rice**
1½ tablespoons **Thai fish sauce**
salt
3–4 **kaffir lime leaves,** finely shredded, to garnish

Heat the oil in a wok or large skillet over medium heat and stir-fry the curry paste for 3–4 minutes or until fragrant. Add the pork and stir-fry for 4–5 minutes.

Add the beans and sugar, stir-fry for 4–5 minutes, then add the rice and fish sauce and stir-fry for another 3–4 minutes. Season to taste, divide among 4 warmed serving plates, and garnish with shredded lime leaves.

For rice with spicy vegetables, heat 1 tablespoon peanut oil in a large wok or skillet over medium heat and stir-fry 2–3 tablespoons Thai red curry paste for 3–4 minutes or until fragrant. Add 6 cups sugarsnap peas and 16 baby corn and stir-fry for 3–4 minutes. Add 5 cups cold cooked jasmine rice and 2–2½ tablespoons light soy sauce and stir-fry for another 3–4 minutes or until the rice has just warmed through. Serve immediately.

tomato & fennel rice

Serves **4**

Preparation time **20 minutes**, plus soaking and standing

Cooking time **about 20 minutes**

1 ½ cups **basmati rice**

3 tablespoons **sunflower oil**

4 **shallots**, finely chopped

2 teaspoons **fennel seeds**

2 **garlic cloves**, finely chopped

4 ripe **tomatoes**, skinned, seeded and finely chopped

2 cups **hot water**

2 tablespoons finely chopped fresh **cilantro**

salt and **black pepper**

Wash the rice several times in cold water, then let soak for 15 minutes. Drain thoroughly.

Heat the oil in a heavy saucepan and sauté the shallots, fennel, and garlic for 4—5 minutes. Add the tomatoes and rice and stir-fry for 2—3 minutes. Season well and pour in the measured hot water. Cover tightly, reduce the heat, and simmer gently for 10 minutes. Do not lift the lid because the steam is required for the cooking process.

Remove the pan from the heat and let the rice stand, covered and undisturbed, for 8—10 minutes. Fluff up the grains with a fork, stir in the fresh cilantro, and serve immediately.

For cherry tomato & almond rice, replace the fennel seeds with an equal quantity of coarsely crushed coriander seeds and use 16 halved cherry tomatoes instead of diced tomatoes. When you fluff up the rice, add 2 tablespoons toasted slivered almonds.

index